Rednecks and Barbarians

"For anyone who wants to learn more about French decolonial theory and to read one of the most interesting antiracist decolonial activists in France today, Houria Bouteldja. Known for her incisive analysis of moral antiracism in France, Bouteldja offers here a strong argument for the unity between 'rednecks' and 'barbarians'. This is essential to fight the foundations of the total racial state and its racial pact which maintains the division between these two groups."

—Françoise Vergès, author of *A Programme of Absolute Disorder: Decolonizing the Museum*

"Houria Bouteldja throws all our certainties into the air, and with brilliant precision, reassembles them. With a clear and uncompromising eye, she points towards a truly emancipatory future in which, following Fanon, all the Wretched of the Earth can 'look for something else', far beyond the racial state."

—Alana Lentin, author of *Why Race Still Matters*

"A masterpiece."

—François Bégaudeau, author of *The Class*

Praise for the author:

"The hatred that Houria Bouteldja arouses is commensurate with her courage."

—Annie Ernaux

"Courageous and controversial."

—Cornel West

Rednecks and Barbarians

Uniting the White and Racialized Working Class

Houria Bouteldja

Translated by Rachel Valinsky

PLUTO  PRESS

First published by La Fabrique éditions 2023

English language edition first published 2024 by Pluto Press
New Wing, Somerset House, Strand, London WC2R 1LA
and Pluto Press, Inc.
1930 Village Center Circle, 3-834, Las Vegas, NV 89134

www.plutobooks.com

British Library Cataloguing in Publication Data
A catalogue record for this book is available from the British Library

ISBN   978 0 7453 4955 8   Paperback
ISBN   978 0 7453 4957 2   PDF
ISBN   978 0 7453 4956 5   EPUB

This book is printed on paper suitable for recycling and made from fully
managed and sustained forest sources. Logging, pulping and manufacturing
processes are expected to conform to the environmental standards of the
country of origin.

Typeset by Stanford DTP Services, Northampton, England

Simultaneously printed in the United Kingdom and United States of America

Contents

To my mother, who does not disarm

In memory of Éric Hazan, my French publisher,
who believed in me and without whom this book would not exist

In memory of Madame Cocchi, Madame Bal,
and Catherine Grupper

Introduction

The angel Gabriel asked: "Inform me about the hour ... Tell me some of its indications," and the Prophet replied: "That you will find barefooted, destitute goat-herds vying with one another in the construction of magnificent buildings."[1]
—Hadith, transmitted by Muslim

The nations were angry, and your wrath has come. The time has come ... for destroying those who destroy the earth.[2]
—The Apocalypse of St. John the Apostle

It's the end of the world.

The Torah, the Bible, and the Qur'an all foretold it.

Try as we might to scan the horizon, only darkened skies and gloomy suns appear. All the warning signs are flashing. I'd like to talk about hope, but I can feel the word falling out of fashion.

It's the end of the world. Our fundamental certainties, our modern conception of unlimited material, moral, and ethical progress, are no more. Whether because of the threat of nuclear war, of viruses, or of climate change, there is no utopia, however desirable, that could still prevail over our lucidity and resignation.

The most secular and scientific minds are beginning to agree with the believers. They now share a common imaginary: the end is nigh.

This is a good start. But let's go further and consider the power of negative thinking. Let's consider its power and use it as support. Not to accelerate this end, but to render back to despair its metaphysical dimension. Hope is no longer what keeps us alive, despair is. Now, that's a concrete, materialist perspective ... the end of the world as

---

1 TN: "Muslim 8a," in The Book of Faith, last accessed June 11, 2024, https://sunnah.com/muslim:8a.
2 TN: Revelation 11:18 (New International Version).

a mobilizing myth and even as the basis for a newfound positive awareness. Didn't the poet say, "Where there is danger, / also grows the saving power"?[3]

The world is dead, long live the world!

While the end of the world is certain in all monotheistic religions, the hour at which it will come remains a secret. A secret that modern man, more than any other creature on earth, has attempted to uncover. While the end of the world now seems so near, it could still be differed, provided our collective will is to be done with the world *as it exists.*

This world is capitalistic. This world is the destruction of the living. This world is war. We must put an end to it. Now.

But while capitalism is everywhere, the nations most responsible for the end of the world are, in large part, located in the West. This is where I'm writing from, from the heart of French capitalism. This is where my despair flourishes. It is here that my hope must be reborn, from here that I must contemplate the end of *this* world.

As I face the challenge of holding the line amid the ruins of political hope, I might as well remain realistic and demand the impossible, right? The impossible will be: the end of *this* world. A NEW HOPE.

We've got the Idea, the mobilizing myth. We know who the Enemy is. Now, what we need is a collective will and an overall strategy to "destroy those who destroy the earth." But this is where things get complicated, because the grassroots forces capable of putting an end to this world are disunited, divided, even opposed to one another. The wager is to find a way to unite them. The reasons for this disunity are many, but among the most structural, the oldest, and the most effective is the racial divide. It is that entanglement which this book considers.

Must one be mad to persist in believing in the formation of a historical bloc capable of organizing and resisting against, even gaining the upper hand over, the enemy? A bloc that would be successful in uniting its working classes and armed with a strategy for con-

---

3   Friedrich Hölderlin, "Patmos" (1803), trans. Scott Horton, *Harper's Magazine*, July 16, 2007, last accessed June 11, 2024, https://harpers.org/2007/07/patmos/.

quering power and the State? If any such unity is asserting itself and being proclaimed as triumphant, it is that of white supremacy—the last and ultimate recourse of the Western bourgeois bloc, which has been shaken from all sides by the social and political crises it continues to provoke and aggravate day after day. We await the *big one*, that deflagration of a scale unknown (the end?), which we anticipate will be immense. From this point of view, France is a textbook case, but our understanding of what is happening to us cannot do without an analysis of capitalism as a *totality*. Any Marxist worthy of the name knows this well, but it is worth reiterating the main points here. Such an analysis must first and foremost situate the French State and its policies within the global world—the "world-system," as Wallerstein would call it[4]—in which economic powers compete. This world is a combination of economic dynamics dominated by financial capital and geopolitical logics, which are imposed on any State by virtue of its participation in this imperialist global world. In the twentieth century, two episodes disrupted the world-system, leaving an indelible and traumatic mark on advanced capitalist countries: the Russian Revolution and the liberation struggles of the Third World. But since the collapse of the USSR, most geopolitical obstacles have fallen away. Capital enjoys the unlimited freedom to exploit people, land, and the environment. With the demise of the "evil empire," it became necessary to find a new enemy against which the imperialist bloc could unite. The Iranian Revolution, the rise of political Islam, and then the jihadist attacks provided an opportunity for the ideological basis of this unity to develop. For this war requires the national unity of the people with their rulers or, to put it another way, the alliance of the bourgeoisie and the white subaltern classes against the Wretched of the Earth abroad, and against the indigenous at home.[5] As long as there is popular consensus, the forces of

---

4   TN: Immanuel Wallerstein, *The Modern World-System*, 4 vols (New York/San Diego: Academic Press; Berkeley: University of California Press, 1974–2011).

5   TN: The category "indigenous" is a key concept for Bouteldja and the antiracist, decolonial Parti des Indigènes de la République (Party of the Indigenous of the Republic, or PIR, founded in 2005), of which she was a member until 2020. Bouteldja defines the indigenous of the Republic as the "population living in

law and order, the police, and the army stay out of public life and let the government arbitrate. But if consensus erodes, as trends of mass absenteeism and social revolt tend to indicate, the army can become autonomous and "take charge."

It is in this context—in which the radical left and political anti-racism have become irrelevant, the social democracy that once acted as a shock absorber has been liquidated, the far right is thriving, and the topics of immigration and Islam are taking center stage in public debate—that we urgently need to update our analyses of the State and of the biological nature of race as a technology for the organization of society.

Such will be the first ambition of this book.

*   *   *

Is racism a passion of the elites, as Jacques Rancière suggests, or, on the contrary, a passion of the "proles," as a large part of the Republican political field, particularly on the left, seems to think? Is there, as a number of activists and researchers like Fabrice Dhume and Éric Fassin claim, such a thing as State racism, as a racist State?

My thesis is that race is indissociable from the formation of modern States. Consequently, the argument that consists in opposing "top-down racism" to "bottom-up racism," or that exonerates the State by turning racism into a conjunctural variable, is beside the point: there is a dialectical relationship between the two that Gramsci's idea of the "integral State" can help us understand.

Gramsci defines the "integral State" as a "hegemony protected by the armour of coercion" and comprising the state apparatuses of

---

France whose origins are in the former French colonies as well as France's current overseas colonies. Forged by activists from within colonial immigrant communities in France, this concept refers to the category 'Indigenous' as deployed by republican France in the nineteenth and twentieth centuries to designate its colonial subjects …. In so far as this category has been resignified and reclaimed, it describes, in the PIR's estimation, "both State policy and the subjectivities of those who in fact refuse the inferiorized status that the State assigns to them." See Houria Bouteldja, "Party of the Indigenous of the Republic (PIR) Key Concepts," trans. Paola Bacchetta, *Critical Ethnic Studies* 1, no. 1 (Spring 2015): 30–1.

"political society" and "civil society."[6] It is a dialectical unity consisting of the formations of civil society and political society, the "entire complex of practical and theoretical activities by which the ruling class not only justifies and maintains its domination but manages to obtain the active consent of those over whom it rules."[7] But what is the role of race in all this? I propose to demonstrate that the "integral State" is an integral *racial* State.[8] It has been difficult for this idea to gain traction in France, where it is met with much resistance, whereas in other countries it is, at the very least, a subject of debate: racial States exist, and the French State is among them. Indeed, while Gérard Noiriel, René Gallissot, and Suzanne Citron have masterfully described the mechanisms that—since the French Revolution, and especially since the Third Republic—have "nationalized the French people" through a social/national pact, and while numerous Marxist thinkers including Nicos Poulantzas and Antonio Gramsci have theorized the capitalist State, this analysis lacks a racial basis, especially with regards to the French State. Establishing this fact will also enable us to study the relationship that has developed between the State, political society, and civil society in France over the past two centuries through the prism of race.

Gramsci never claimed to turn the State, "civil society," and "political society" into absolutes that elude history. He himself recognized that these were "methodological" distinctions, not "organic" ones. I take this opportunity to signal that I too will be taking liberties with Gramsci's definition of these terms. First, I will take up Poulantzas's notion according to which "the State is not a monolithic bloc, but a strategic field"[9] that "regulates not only the relationship of forces

---

6   TN: Antonio Gramsci, *Selections from the Prison Notebooks*, ed. Quintin Hoare and Geoffrey Nowell Smith (New York: International Publishers, 1971), 263.
7   TN: Ibid., 244.
8   The purpose of this book is not to prove the existence of racial States (although I devote the first chapter to this), as this issue has already been amply discussed by experts in the field. See David Theo Goldberg's *The Racial State* (Malden, MA: Wiley-Blackwell, 2002), which has not been translated into French but is a classic in the English-speaking world.
9   TN: Nicos Poulantzas, *State, Power, Socialism* (London: Verso, 2014 [1978]), 138.

between fractions of the power bloc, but also the relationship between the power bloc and the dominated classes."[10] Next, I will focus my analysis of "political society" on political organizations and unions, which constitute a class-based opposition to the ruling bloc. Finally, "civil society" will be considered under the murky category of "the people," and its constituent unit in modern States, "the citizen."

It won't be long before this approach is criticized as too mechanistic, too systematic—and that critique wouldn't be entirely wrong. While I argue here that the prism of race is both absolutely essential and perpetually obscured, this is not to make assumptions about other historical determinisms subject to other logics. Race is one dimension of history, not all of it.

My second ambition, which is also a Gramscian one, is not to give up on "optimism of the will" and on utopia, an expression so overused that it has lost its revolutionary force. I'd like to breathe new life into it here. The idea is as follows: the integral (racial) State, however tentacular, does not exhaust either the human being or their capacity to break their chains and enjoy their freedom. Inside the diving bell, there is a butterfly. This butterfly loves life and dreams only of one thing: escape. How else are we to understand the Sardinian revolutionaries' optimism of the will? And how could this not become the philosophical substrate of every political strategy? Or, to put it another way, how can we hope to overturn the forms of capitalist exploitation without first *believing*? Without believing that a faith, an objective, and a strategy can produce a new political community, a revolutionary "we"? To this end, I needed to identify two revolutionary subjects: Rednecks[11] and Barbarians. "Rednecks" and

---

10   TN: Paul Costello on Nicos Poulantzas in "Capitalism, the State and Crises," *Theoretical Review*, no. 20 (January–February 1981), last accessed June 11, 2024, www.marxists.org/history/erol/ncm-7/19812001.htm.

11   TN: The titular word *beauf* has been translated, in this book, by the word "redneck." While this invariably gestures to a distinct geographic context (the United States), and to a pejorative stereotype of the poor, white, uneducated, and prejudiced/racist rural working class (dating back to the nineteenth century, the term grows out of the sunburn found on farmers' necks due to long hours

"Barbarians" are not my terms. They are the terms of class contempt and racism. They are the terms employed by the principal enemy. The terms in which that enemy has imprisoned the white proletariat, on the one hand, and the indigenous proletariat on the other—two groups whose political potential that enemy is aware of and has successfully opposed and neutralized, often with the complicity of some of the very same people concerned. The result: "rednecks" say "they" when speaking about "barbarians," and conversely, "barbarians" say "they" when speaking about "rednecks." The project, then, is to replace the word "they" with the word "we."

I'll admit, "we" is a strange word.

It is both diabolical and improbable. At a time when "I's" and "me's" are brandished on all sides and the "we's" of white supremacy are thriving, this word seems almost incongruous. All the more so when you consider that the various constituents and sub-constituents of this great Fanonian "we" are almost all more unknowable than the next. A white working-class "we"? Unlikely. An indigenous "we"? What a joke. The encounter between these two "we's": a mirage. Their union within a historical bloc? A chimera. So, I set out to write a book that was, in my own eyes, almost unjustifiable, clinging to the fragile branch of that popular adage, which is as accurate as it is derisory: "where there is life there is hope." A NEW HOPE. For while I have great difficulty convincing myself that such a unity is possible, I cannot resign myself to the idea that everything has been attempted. We must start, then, with what is in the way.

Chin up!

---

of working outdoors), "redneck" also shores up a history of labor and activist movements in the Appalachian region of the United States. From the 1877 Railroad Strike in West Virginia to the violent suppression of an interracial coalition of coal miners attempting to unionize at Blair Mountain, West Virginia, in 1921, "redneck" was used as an epithet to designate workers who wore a red bandana as a symbol of union solidarity. Of many of the other possible terms cycled through as possible translations of the word *beauf*, the dual trajectories of the "redneck" felt most appropriate, if inadequate, approximations of the term for an anglophone context.

ASIDE

The year is 1920. Captain Perrin has received an order to look for the remains of a "poilu"[12] whose fate is to be honored as the Unknown Soldier under the Arc de Triomphe.

Major Dellaplane: "Perrin, be very careful!"

Perrin: "Yes, I know, I know, no English or Germans."

Dellaplane: "And no negroes either."

Later, in a village where the search takes place:

A villager: "All the soldiers who are buried here are ours. Along the road to the Roberts', they're mostly Krauts. Or Arabs and two Belgians.

Perrin: "There are Arabs too?"

The villager: "Only Arabs toward the end! Except for the officers."

Perrin: "What I'm looking for, m'am, is a French soldier. Really French. And anonymous."

The villager: "The one next to the well. A grenade exploded in his hand, the poor man. His name was Mounier, he was from Le Mans."

Perrin: "Anonymous, Madam! An-nonymous. A soldier with no name, no identity. An unknown soldier."

The villager: "Unknown? But we knew them all a little."

—Scenes from Bertrand Tavernier, *Life and Nothing But* (1989)

---

12   TN: Translating literally as "the hairy one," the term was to refer to French infantrymen during the First World War.

PART I

The Integral Racial State,
or Pessimism of the Intellect

The Racial State

Only a moral idea still stands, namely the fact that one cannot be both poet and Ambassador to France.

—Surrealists[1]

The definition of the State as racial—among other things—cannot be grasped in its essence without a firm grounding in a clear theoretical perspective. Here, I will discuss only the modern formation of the State, born of the womb of Western modernity, which Sadri Khiari defines as a historical globality characterized by Capital, colonial/postcolonial domination, the modern State, and the hegemonic system of ethics associated with it.[2]

While the primitive accumulation of capital predates the emergence of modernity, it is its transatlantic expansion that determined the conditions and modalities of its development. Marx himself agrees:

The discovery of the gold and silver in America, the extirpation, enslavement and entombment in mines of the aboriginal popula-

---

1 Open letter to Mr. Paul Claudel, French Ambassador to Japan, July 1, 1925, signed by Maxime Alexandre, Louis Aragon, Antonin Artaud, J.-A. Boiffard, Joë Bousquet, André Breton, Jean Carrive, René Crevel, Robert Desnos, Paul Eluard, Max Ernst, T. Fraenkel, Francis Gérard, Eric de Haulleville, Michel Leiris, Georges Limbour, Mathias Lübeck, Georges Malkine, André Masson, Max Morise, Marcel Noll, Benjamin Péret, Georges Ribemont-Dessaignes, Philippe Soupault, Dédé Sunbeam, Roland Tual, Jacques Viot, and Roger Vitrac.
2 TN: See Houria Bouteldja, "Race, classe et genre: une nouvelle divinité à trois têtes," Le Parti des Indigènes de la République (PIR), December 14, 2015, last accessed June 11, 2024, https://indigenes-republique.fr/race-classe-et-genre-une-nouvelle-divinite-a-trois-tetes-2/; and Houria Bouteldja and Youssef Boussoumah, "The Parti des Indigènes de la République—a Political Success and the Conspiracy Against It (2005 to 2020)," Verso (blog), October 6, 2021, last accessed June 11, 2024, www.versobooks.com/blogs/news/5167-the-parti-des-indigenes-de-la-republique-a-political-success-and-the-conspiracy-against-it-2005-to-2020/.

tion, the beginning of the conquest and looting of the East Indies, the turning of Africa into a warren for the commercial hunting of black-skins, signalised the rosy dawn of the era of capitalist production. These idyllic proceedings are the chief momenta of primitive accumulation.[3]

Within the capitalist mode of production class, race, and gender have developed as technologies of social organization integrated into modern-States-in-formation and placed at the service of the ruling classes to increase exploitation, divide the social body, and consolidate and reproduce their own power. Each of these technologies played its part in the extraction of surplus value and in social organization on a global scale as capitalism deployed itself.

Race relations involve theft, the appropriation of land and resources, and the rape and killing of "people of color," with the ultimate goal of appropriating incalculable riches ahead of the production process.[4] This is pure accumulation, and it is foundational to the very principle of colonization of the Americas, Africa, and Asia. Enslavement and free labor followed. The owner purchases a slave in the same way he would purchase a tool or a machine; it's an investment, and he will later extract maximum surplus value through that unpaid labor. The enslaved person belongs to the master, who has the right of life or death over them and feeds them only to reproduce their labor power. In the history of the world, slavery has been applied to all kinds of populations, whatever their origin, skin color, or religion, but under the capitalist regime, it first and foremost concerned Black people, and later, "people of color." Over time and across space, race became a means of extracting surplus value—increasingly remunerated, to be sure, but competitive with the surplus value extracted from the white proletariat, both within and outside the nation-state.

---

3   Karl Marx, "Genesis of the Industrial Capitalist" (Part 3, Chapter 31), in *Capital: A Critique of Political Economy*, vol. 1, *The Process of Capitalist Production*, ed. Frederick Angels, trans. Samuel Moore and Edward Aveling (Chicago, IL: Charles H. Kerr & Company, 1932), 823.
4   More specifically, as Marx writes, force "is itself an economic power." Ibid., 824.

Class relations involve a compromise that materializes through a sales and purchase agreement. The employer purchases labor power in exchange for remuneration. Here, labor power is a commodity that produces surplus value, enabling another form of capital accumulation. The worker is dispossessed of the means of production, which belong to the employer. This class relation is one that has historically bound white employers to white workers; the employer must concede a share, albeit negligible, of their profit. This is the radical distinction between the slave and the worker.

Gender relations are implicit, non-formalized relations connecting a woman and her husband's employer. Under the capitalist regime, the woman's role is to reproduce labor power. She feeds the worker, does his laundry, and relieves him emotionally and sexually. She gives birth to the future workforce and does so *without remuneration*. The work she performs free of charge in exchange for the room and board provided by her husband represents an extraction of surplus value that increases capitalist margins. Materialist and Marxist feminists have extensively documented this phenomenon as "an aspect ... that led to the establishment of capitalism in Europe."[5]

These three technologies of wealth extraction are articulated in a complex entanglement that will vary over time as capital mutates yet continue to inform and structure the world today. The extraction of surplus value has never been as proficient as it is under the capitalist regime, which owes its longevity, efficiency, and coherence only to its ability to structure relations of exploitation on a global scale and adapt them to the balance of power in place at a local and international level.

Thus, in the pages that follow, there will be no trace of the primacy of race over class (or gender). One could even argue that race is a modality of class (and gender), just as class is a modality of race (and gender). It follows that racial struggle is a modality of class struggle.

---

5   Silvia Federici, *Witches, Witch-Hunting, and Women* (Oakland, CA: PM Press, 2018), 13. The witch-hunts of the sixteenth and seventeenth centuries constitute an offensive led by a fledgling capitalism to control reproduction.

It also follows that class struggle is a modality of racial struggle. It is all a matter of time, space, and conjunctural frame. It is important to dispel the false objection that one takes precedence over the others.

All decolonial theorists agree that 1492 marks the historical transition to modernity; and this moment, it must be noted, preceded not only the Industrial Revolution—of which it is a precondition—but also, consequently, the formation of the European and American mass proletariat.[6] While it is out of the question here to privilege race over class, it is nevertheless imperative to situate the development of these two forms of social organization within a historical chronology. Let's state it from the outset: without race, there can be no post-industrial working class. In this respect, it must also be stated that race and its socio-historical expression—racism—did not appear all of a sudden with the "discovery" of the Americas. At the risk of shocking people, one could even say that the genocide of autochtonous peoples,[7] just like the transatlantic deportation and enslavement of Africans, did not yet constitute *racism*, even if its seeds could already be found in Reconquista Spain under the guise of Christianity's domination over Islam and Judaism. These are, without a doubt, acts of infinite barbarity. But neither barbarity nor cruelty were new phenomena in the fifteenth century.

"An act of cruelty in the tenth century is exactly as cruel, neither more nor less so, than an act of cruelty in the nineteenth."[8]

The history of mankind attests to the fact that such cruelties are not the prerogative of the European peoples, who, it's true, had already undergone a particularly bloody history.

Thus, the concepts of "barbarism" and "inhumanity" will not be employed here. Only racism will be considered as a mode of expro-

---

6 Even though in Europe, there had been, since the sixteenth century, an ongoing process of proletarianization fueled by the violent expropriation of the countrysides. They formed the semislave labor force sent to the Americas.

7 TN: This translation preserves the author's use of the term "autochthonous" as distinct from her formulation of the political category "indigenous."

8 Simone Weil, *The Need for Roots: Prelude to a Declaration of Duties towards Mankind*, trans. Arthur Wills (London: Routledge, 2002), 223.

priation or exploitation mobilized by the State and its apparatuses, and as a modality of domination forged by the dominating class.

Nonetheless, the deportations, genocides, massacres, mass displacements, rapes, and pillages of non-European peoples served as the historical foundation for the racial determination of States-in-formation. They took for granted the absolutely derisory nature of this humanity, which cannot yet be described retroactively as non-white, but which would progressively become so by force of circumstance. It was necessary to identify who would be the recipients of the distribution of wealth and who would be deprived of it, either through spoliation, exploitation, or elimination. Only the modern State would have the power to meet this challenge, for not only was it necessary to classify and hierarchize humanity, it was also necessary to contain the insatiable rage and revolt of the excluded—a category constantly being defined and redefined by the mutations of capital that accompany revolutions and counter-revolutions. In other words, the struggle of the Wretched of the Earth—which I like to think of as a powerful driving force of history—had to be contained and restrained. Numerous concessions of "reason" had to be made, concessions that would progressively separate "people of color" from white workers until they became antagonistic entities. Newly formed racial States initially accomplished this by naturalizing their uncompromising exploitation of non-Whites, and would continue to do so until the nineteenth century. These same racial States, under pressure from revolts, competition between colonialist States, and the mutations of capital, would produce the nation-states and nationalism that have come to define them since the nineteenth century.

But, let us study the formation of the racial State more clinically. Let us consider, from the outset, that such a State is entirely strategic, and that its ruling forces know they do not fully control it. These forces also know they must constantly ensure that antagonisms (whether internal to the bourgeois bloc or emanating from the exploited) do not jeopardize their hegemony. It will become clear, then, that this State is not doomed to be capitalistic, that it is a site of confrontation for power relations, and that these can be overturned. We owe the birth, development, and perpetuation of the racial State to this fear. Let's begin here.

PREHISTORY OF THE RACIAL STATE

The famous Valladolid Debate—"do Indians possess a soul?"— which took place in Spain under Charles V in the mid-sixteenth century and would determine the degree of humanity of the natives of the "New World," is in some sense the paradigm through which the white world has approached the question of race up until the present day.

"There is no racism without theory (or theories)," says Balibar.[9]

Let's consider this debate (between aspiring Whites) as the original matrix of racialist theory. Indeed, the joust between the Dominican Bartolomé de las Casas, a friend of the "indigenous people," and the theologian Juan Ginés de Sepulveda, their enemy, serves as a template: it will, of course, undergo transformations as history unfolds, yet it contains the ideological justification for all political formations of Western modernity, be they absolute or par-liamentary monarchies, democratic republics, or fascist regimes; be they European, American, Canadian, South African, or Australian. This template is foundational to the ideological architecture of cap-italist modernity, which would establish the psychic structures of Christian and European domination, while also ensuring what one might call "the security of conscience." In short, this debate would perpetually swing from its hard-edged version of assertive racism to its soft version of paternalistic humanism. While both sides decried their victory at the end of the controversy, the condemnation of the enslavement of "Indians," placed under the protection of the Crown, was quickly transgressed under pressure from groups defending economic interests. This condemnation also served as a pretext for the owning classes to seek free labor elsewhere: Africa.

---

9   TN: Étienne Balibar, "Is There a 'Neo-Racism'?" trans. Chris Turner, in Étienne Balibar and Immanuel Wallerstein, *Race, Nation, Class: Ambiguous Identities* (London: Verso, 1991), 19.

At the time of the debate, most of the actors were already in place, even though history hadn't yet molded them into the players we recognize today: the white proletariat did not yet exist, but the European colonizing power was there, as was the mass of autochthonous workers who would have to be made into slaves or employees soon enough. It wasn't all played out at the time, and it was too early to assert, as David Theo Goldberg has done, with the benefit of historical hindsight, that the modern State is nothing if not a racial State.[10] However, the foundations of this State were laid: from the outset, race played a structuring role. The racial State would continue to oscillate between "naturalist" and "historicist" approaches.[11] The former advanced a biological, hereditary conception of race, while the latter took a progressive stance according to which the indigenous could reform themselves. While the indigenous were considered primitive, their encounter with Europe could liberate them from this condition. As we shall see, these two seemingly mutually exclusive conceptions were merely strategic adaptations of the capitalist mode to the challenges of history and of social transformations and struggles, or, as Sadri Khiari writes, different "ideological ... modes of existence of the *struggle between social races*."[12] The former dominated until the nineteenth century, while the latter gained momentum with the emergence of industrial society and nation-

---

10   See David Theo Goldberg, *The Racial State* (Malden, MA: Wiley-Blackwell, 2002).

11   Ibid.

12   TN: Sadri Khiari, *The Colonial Counter-Revolution in France: From de Gaulle to Sarkozy*, trans. Amos Hodges (South Pasadena, CA: Semiotext(e), 2021), 27. The concept of "social races" as theorized by Bouteldja and Khiari (a member of the Party of the Indigenous of the Republic), "designates indivisibly the social relation of oppression and resistance to oppression produced by the process of racialization linked to capitalist coloniality and social groups that are hierarchized in function of defined statues based on phenotypical, cultural, and racialized religious criteria. Social races are only incarnated as such through the social conflict that defines limits and power and thus they can only be plural. By definition, social races only exist in relation to each other." See Houria Bouteldja, "Party of the Indigenous of the Republic (PIR) Key Concepts," trans. Paola Bacchetta, *Critical Ethnic Studies* 1, no. 1 (Spring 2015): 28.

states—signal superstructures of the capitalist world-system. Let's start with the former.

THE NATURALIST RACIAL STATE

According to the Valladolid paradigm, the embryonic State—owing to a balance of power that favored the conquistadores, who agreed with Sepulveda's theory—would initially be *naturalist*. Is it any coincidence that the modern era was inaugurated by genocide? On the whole, even though the production of alterities specific to pre-modern periods did exist, notably in Europe or among the Hellenes, pre-capitalist expansions and conquests did not assimilate or exclude. They massacred and burned, but carved few alterities into stone:

> [T]he Greeks and Romans, Islam and the Crusaders, Attila and Tamerlane all killed in order to clear a path in an open, continuous and already homogenous space; that accounts for the undifferentiated massacres which marked the exercise of power in the great nomadic empires. Genocide becomes possible only when the national space is closed on *foreign* bodies within its very frontiers.[13]

While the nation-state was still a distant project, genocide and its justification—they do not have a soul, they are not Christian—constitute a project to occupy land through the expulsion of natives, as well as through their identification as other. This othering was naturalized from the start. "Indians" are savages. They are beings in a state of nature, fixed in time, incapable of evolving, timeless, and one with nature. This logic, which imposes an ahistoric, racial determination on indigenous people, prefigures the naturalist character of the modern State during its formation process. This would move Rousseau many years later, as he glanced back at the colonial past:

---

13   Nicos Poulantzas, *State, Power, Socialism* (London: Verso, 2014 [1978]), 120.

It is something extremely remarkable that, for the many years that the Europeans torment themselves in order to acclimate the savages of various countries to their lifestyle, they have not yet been able to win over a single one of them, not even by means of Christianity; for our missionaries sometimes turn them into Christians, but never into civilized men.[14]

It is hardly surprising that the fate reserved to the natives, and later, to Africans, served as a perfect template for Hitler and Mussolini.

If the savage had to be fixed in their nature thus, it was because the political and economic power being formed had to acquire a supervisory and political capacity, as well as a strong sense of self. Defining, classifying, and hierarchizing quickly became ways of exercising power that could be generalized and mobilized if necessary by the armed forces of coercion. Maintaining order, security, and control is the primary function of any State. The reasons for this are manifold, but above all economic: to control resources and land, accumulate wealth, and create a labor force that can be exploited at will.

The State precedes race. It gives birth to it. It delivers it all the more hastily, having been formed in a dominant culture that cut its teeth on the Jews and Muslims of Spain, in a psychic environment that already took for granted pre-racial forms of othering. The State gives birth to race out of immediate necessity, for how can it make a small number of people richer when there are so many human beings claiming their share. The State gives birth to race because settlers were already animated by a spirit of ownership. So, the debate about the souls of indigenous people is anything but trivial. It sowed the seeds of the concept of race. One could even say that race is the primitive state of class as we know it since the nineteenth century.[15] At its foundation was the slave trade. Driven by an

---

14 Jean-Jacques Rousseau, "Discourse on the Origin of Inequality," in *Basic Political Writings of Jean-Jacques Rousseau*, ed. and trans. Donald A. Cress (Indianapolis: Hackett Publishing Company, 1987), 106.
15 Insofar as the primitive (or primary) accumulation of capital took place, in part, (not only) through (racial) colonization, class, "in its primitive state," is organized along racial lines.

irrepressible, predatory impulse, but constrained by various royal decrees protecting indigenous people, the Spanish inaugurated the era of racial slavery and the plantationocene.[16] Colossal fortunes were built on the forced labor of millions of Africans and on the trade of plantation products that marked the true rise of capitalism. There was also the intensification of competition between the powers of that time, which remain the powers of the Western bloc today: Holland, England, and France. It is to these powers that we owe the constitution of the first racial States, which set in motion the most lucrative trade of their day. We can say, following Wallerstein, that "race and racism unifies intrazonally the core zones and the peripheral zones in their battles with each other,"[17] and that the role of States was to organize the market both at a legal level and at an economic and political level. Each of these countries followed the path of economic liberalism, which would become a veritable political philosophy. The toughest among them were also those to demonstrate the fiercest attachment to the institution of slavery.

Liberalism was first introduced to the American colonies by the Dutch, who supplanted the Spanish and inaugurated the slave trade on a large scale. Long before the English and French, the Dutch bourgeoisie broke with the Ancien Régime and the feudal system and set out to conquer the world, establishing its first colonies. Holland became the political and ideological center of Europe, where the first great liberal minds were forged. As the bourgeoisie was "the first … [class] in history to need a corps of *organic intellectuals* in order to establish itself as the dominant class,"[18] it was in Holland that the earliest writings of Bernard de Mandeville and John Locke, the fathers of economic liberalism, emerged. It was also in Holland that Descartes's *Discourse on Method* was published—the volume in

---

16 This term refers to the geologic era that began with the colonization of the Americas, which is marked by human impact on the biosphere and climate. See Malcolm Ferdinand, *Decolonial Ecology: Thinking from the Caribbean World*, trans. Anthony Paul Smith (Cambridge: Polity Press, 2022).

17 TN: Immanuel Wallerstein, "The Construction of Peoplehood: Racism, Nationalism, Ethnicity," in Balibar and Wallerstein, *Race, Nation, Class*, 87.

18 Poulantzas, *State, Power, Socialism*, 72.

which first appeared the famous "I think, therefore I am," which liberation philosopher Enrique Dussel interpreted as a confession: "I conquer, therefore I am." England, after its "Glorious Revolution," stole Holland's thunder, wresting away its monopoly on slavery.

If there is one feature that characterizes the liberals of that time, it is, without a doubt, their consensus on slavery. These liberals were as fiercely opposed to taxation, which they equated with despotism, as they were passionately in favor of free trade and slavery. But it was also this passion for slavery that put an end to British dominion over its colonies, which would emancipate themselves by carrying out their own revolutions. The unity of the English "nation" was broken as settlers denounced "enslavement" as well as their subordination to the Crown. "Negro hunters" declared their independence in the name of absolute freedom, liberal ideology, and inalienable rights, which they categorically denied to Black people. The United States were born and built their independence on this foundation: economic liberalism, the dispossession of indigenous people, and slavery. Every State to come into being after the Declaration of Independence of the United States of America of July 4, 1776, was built on this consensus. Racial States were definitively established at that time, and would continue, to this day, to complexify their political, legal, and military arsenal to preserve and optimize the racial order.

The nineteenth century saw the rise of the Industrial Revolution and a new chapter in the history of triumphant capitalism. This was the century of the territorial colonization of Africa, which became a major supplier of raw materials for both France and England. Africa was violently integrated into a global capitalist system dominated by Europeans, who seized most of the wealth produced. Racial ideology was in full swing. Plundered and enslaved peoples were "inferior." By the end of the nineteenth century, the colonial experience was shared by all the peoples of the Global South: China, India, Indonesia, and the Arab world.

You'll forgive me this familiar detour into colonial history, but it's important to understand that it was the pressure of capitalism—which knows no temporal or spatial bounds—as well as the competition between national bourgeoisies, that defined the contours of States and their role in the modes of production. It is the State that orders the field of struggle, organizes the market, and delineates the social division of labor—just as it delineates the *racial division of labor*.

The naturalist conception of race dominated, and was institutionalized by law, until the nineteenth century. The Code Noir, the founding act of French colonial law, is its most obvious and fully realized expression.[19] From this point of view, the law materialized and legitimized the violence exercised by the State to profit the triangular trade, the owning classes, and the State itself. But to do this, the myth of white racial homogeneity had to be created. In most imperial centers, racialized subjects were on the periphery, in other words, separated from Europeans. However, wherever there was contact and a threat to white racial homogeneity, the State intervened to separate the "races," as it would do on plantations, with segregation in the United States, or during South African apartheid. It did so by using the law, but also through violent means. The modes of governing employed by States can be characterized as racial because, for the naturalist formation of colonial power, the space of dominated societies is a freed space devoted to profit: its inhabitants are either supernumeraries to be eliminated or members of a low-cost labor force. But race here is not just a technique for the expropriation or extraction of surplus value, it is also a weapon of counter-revolution. During the naturalist period in the Americas, nothing predestined European workers (including enslaved people) to ally with the big landowners. Since racial structuration was not completely established or set in stone, and Whites had not been fully produced as a singular category defending particular inter-

---

19 It is interesting to note that the Code Noir was adopted in March 1685 (two years after the death of Colbert, who had introduced it)—the same year that, in October, the Edict of Nantes was revoked, putting an end to the toleration of Protestantism. As Michelle Zancarini-Fournel has stated, "The royal authority of Louis XIV was now supreme, and minorities—minorities of color in the Americas and religious minorities throughout the kingdom—were paying the price." See Zancarini-Fournel, *Les Luttes et les rêves: Une histoire populaire de la France de 1685 à nos jours* (Paris: Zones, 2016), 15. War without, war within!

ests, it was in the best interest of the owning classes to bind the fate of European workers with their own in the face of a possible, dangerous alliance between European workers and slaves. This is how—under the real threat of class unity among enslaved people, who were not yet really Black, and immigrants from Europe, who were not yet really white—the ruling classes made concessions in favor of the migrants, whose social status was thereby elevated. The better off poor European migrants became, the more effective race as a determinant of status became as well. The greater the appeal of being white, the more their separation from Black people became irremediable. From then on, the wages of whiteness[20] would be, in the hands of the legitimated authorities, the most formidable weapon of the counter-revolution, forming a buffer class between the ruling classes and the enslaved—a class subjected to a lesser extortion of the surplus value it produced. This class would be made up of migrants from Europe, fleeing from poverty. Whites in the making.

FROM THE NATURALIST RACIAL STATE TO THE PROGRESSIVE RACIAL STATE

This history was forged through unprecedented violence, but the peoples who were subjugated and put down by force resisted. Their resistance, as we have seen, forced the powers in place to promote the middle classes, themselves fighting for better living conditions. It also led to a strengthening of the legal arsenal that maintained the slave order—this was one of the functions of the Code Noir. However, the slave system had to confront not only the struggles of the enslaved, but also its own contradictions. As early as the nineteenth century, part of the bourgeoisie realized that, in the age of industrialization, wage labor was more efficient and, above all, more profitable than slavery. If the struggle within the State was also a struggle between factions of the bourgeoisie, it was the industrial

---

20 David R. Roediger, *The Wages of Whiteness: Race and the Making of the American Working Class* (London: Verso, 1991).

bourgeoisie that, in this instance, gained the upper hand over the slaveholding bourgeoisie during the Civil War. As soon as the war was over, Congress ratified a constitutional amendment abolishing slavery on December 18, 1865. This victory for the abolitionists can be symbolically considered as a historic moment in the reconfiguration of capital, itself determined by the Industrial Revolution. There was a gradual shift from naturalist racial States to progressive racial States, which had to adapt and address a new challenge: the racial homogeneity within their borders. Indeed, under the pressure of liberation struggles, wars, and the demand for a workforce, races now cohabited within political spaces that had to be reconfigured as "national" to outline new territorial divisions. This new stage in the racialization of States took place at the expense of the regional cultures and traditions of Europe's many populations, and of course, of all non-white people across the planet.

In this respect, the lynchings of Black people in the United States between the end of the nineteenth and the beginning of the twentieth centuries represent the survivance and persistence of white supremacists, who took justice into their own hands, even overrunning official authorities though they benefited from the complacency of law enforcement. This is the part of white supremacism that failed to adapt as it witnessed its absolute domination wither away. Its frustration would fuel the American far right—the radical wing of Western nations' structural whiteness, which functions as a foil against whiteness even as it normalizes it. In this way, racial States sacrificed part of their base and made space for progressivism and the civilizing mission. From this standpoint, Nazism could be considered as an incongruity of the twentieth century, almost like the vestige of a bourgeoisie that is behind the times and incapable of adapting. The German State under Hitler—an exemplary naturalist—was an anachronism confirmed as such by its own defeat. The capitulation of 1945 vindicated the "enlightened" empires and the forces that governed them. Progressive racial States, led by England, the United States, and France, won their wager.

THE FRENCH NATION-STATE, OR THE EMERGENCE OF THE "PROGRESSIVE" RACIAL STATE

Let's take this statement by the Italian Marxist Domenico Losurdo as a starting point for a new understanding of the historical rupture caused by the French Revolution and the development of bourgeois hegemony within the State, at a time when the slave trade was in full swing:

> The history of the West is faced with a paradox. The clear line of demarcation between whites, on the one hand, and blacks and redskins, on the other, was conducive to the development of relations of equality within the white community.[21]

On the eve of the French Revolution, the colony of Saint-Domingue (Haiti) was producing colossal wealth. It was the world's leading producer of sugar and coffee, while its foreign trade represented more than a third of that of metropolitan France. It is even said that one in ten French people made a living from it, either directly or indirectly. This explains the confrontation between Abbé Grégoire, Marat, and Robespierre and a section of the [National] Convention, which refused to abolish slavery. When the Declaration of the Rights of Man was adopted in 1789, slavery was not abolished. And for good reason: the segregationist party in Saint-Domingue took advantage of the revolution to create Whites-only constituent assemblies, while in Paris the colonial lobby pushed through the constitutionalization of slavery in 1791 on the basis of color prejudice. As Césaire reminds us, Antoine Barnave, the leader of the bourgeois revolution, claimed that the Revolution would not be exported to the colonies; more specifically, that men of color, *even if free*, would be excluded from the benefit of political rights.[22] In 1793, the Girondin Convention still refused to abolish slavery, which the

---

21 Domenico Losurdo, *Liberalism: A Counter-History*, trans. Gregory Elliott (London: Verso, 2011), 107.
22 On this subject, see Aimé Césaire, *Toussaint Louverture: La révolution française et le problème colonial* (Paris: Présence africaine, 1961).

Montagnard Convention did in February 1794.[23] However, the slave trade was reestablished in 1802—proof that the counter-revolution was raging among the ruling factions—only to be abolished again in 1815. Slavery was abolished in 1848[24] in all the French colonies. France was undergoing an economic transformation, and through it, the modernization of its State. As in the United States, the bourgeoisie faced new challenges: slave revolts in the colonies, including the victorious Haitian Revolution. What's more, the market for African slaves was waning. The means used to capture them were increasingly costly and dangerous. The price of slaves was on the rise. Faced with these material difficulties, traders had to consider new ways of reproducing labor. The crude slave system was in decline, which explains, in part, why a portion of the bourgeoisie abandoned it. In metropolitan France, incessant insurrectionary movements destabilized power and threatened the interests of the owning classes. All the warning signs were flashing. The people beheaded a king.

Domenico Losurdo's quote takes on its full meaning in this context. The path of egalitarianism presented itself as a compromise, a condition for racial order and unity among Whites. Because, of course, letting go of the colonies was out of the question. And Jaurès would be the last to contest this:

Sad irony of human history … . The fortunes created at Bordeaux, at Nantes, by the slave-trade gave to the bourgeoisie that pride which needed liberty and contributed to human emancipation.[25]

Until now, race in France had been externalized. A community of interest inside the country would now have to be invented to enable capital to continue to expand abroad and conquer markets, and to stabilize the interior. In other words,

---

23 Without compensation for the colonists.
24 With compensation for the colonists.
25 Jean Jaurès, quoted in C. L. R. James, *A History of Pan-African Revolt* (Oakland, CA: PM Press, 2021 [1938]), 38.

Now, through that very movement by which it both marks out frontiers and unifies national space, the State also turns beyond those frontiers towards an irreversible, clearly demarcated space which yet has no end or final horizon. In other words, it seeks to expand markets, capital and territory.[26]

Let us not forget that the conquest of Algeria began in 1830, some forty years after the French Revolution, and that the great period of colonization of Africa was in full swing beginning in the 1870s, at the time of the great revolutionary fever and of the Paris Commune.

According to Gramsci, the hegemony of the bourgeois class was achieved through its ability to transcend its immediate interests and universalize them for the benefit of the subaltern classes, all the while preserving its power of organization, control, and governance. The need to create relations of equality, or rather, relations tending toward equality, thus became all the more imperative as revolutionary momentum and popular demands asserted themselves. This is indeed what happened: beginning in 1789, the French Revolution liquidated the aristocracy to the benefit of the commercial, manufacturing, and, already at that point, financial bourgeoisie. It was time for national unity. The hegemony of the dominant classes within the State could only be assured if they could make the necessary compromises with the subaltern classes. According to Gramsci, this is what the French Jacobins accomplished: unity between the bourgeoisie and the working classes, achieved through the former's ability to temper their immediate material interests to facilitate interclass alliance, an indispensable condition for mass mobilization around universal social demands.[27] The Jacobins' political hegemony was concentrated in their ability to universalize their own demands, while absorbing some of the popular demands. This drastically distinguished them from the ruling castes of the

---

26 Poulantzas, *State, Power, Socialism*, 119.
27 Of course, it took almost a century of struggle for the bourgeoisie to accept the Republican configuration of power, and in this struggle, it was the proletariat that asserted its views (during the revolutions of 1830, 1848, 1871), without, however, being able to carry its momentum through to the end.

pre-revolutionary period, which did not seek to base their domination on the consent of civil society. In other words, the upper classes were able to create an organic relationship between themselves and the subaltern classes, giving rise to a people/nation which they would lead and organize.

This transition from caste corporatism to class hegemony was a veritable revolution within the revolution. It consecrated what Gramsci called the passage from "corporate-economic" demands to "ethico-political" ones.[28] In the wake of the Dutch and British bourgeoisies, this transformative ambition would lead to the development of the modern State and economic liberalism, on the one hand, and political and civil rights, on the other. The notion of the people would create this organic link in the process of hegemonization of bourgeois power. The vagueness of this notion is precisely what endowed it with power by concealing class contradictions in favor of national sentiment. This moment must be considered a key stage in the formation of the racial State, which materialized into what Sadri Khiari has called "the racial pact."[29]

This pact lies at the heart of the Third Republic, a racial and colonial republic par excellence. A Republic that gave birth to the nation-state—the concrete superstructure that condensed new power relations within the State, which are delineated as follows: primacy of the bourgeoisie over the subaltern classes; primacy of the subaltern classes over the inferior races. These asymmetries gave rise to the two major oppositions to the bourgeois bloc: opposition from the emerging working class, which, though it was integrated into the national project, was economically antagonistic to the bourgeois and proletarian nexus; and opposition from the wretched of the earth, who were excluded from the national project and antagonistic to the bourgeois and proletarian nexus by virtue of their role in the international division of labor.

---

28 TN: See Antonio Gramsci: "Analysis of Situations in Relations of Force," in *Selections from the Prison Notebooks*, ed. Quintin Hoare and Geoffrey Nowell Smith (New York: International Publishers, 1971), 1975–84.
29 TN: Khiari, *The Colonial Counter-Revolution*, 51.

The rupture this pact caused within the thousand-year history of human societies—once based on small communitarian units and close-knit relationships—turned the nation-state into the most revolutionary ethico-political phenomenon in contemporary history. It tore the individual away from their tribal habitus, which it supplanted with a national habitus; it took them away from their "mechanical" solidarity to consign them to an "organic" solidarity, to use Durkheim's term.[30] Whereas individuals had been connected to one another by local solidarity economies, the citizen became an abstraction, connected to other citizens through invisible threads (law, rights, currency, the homeland, which henceforth had to be defended against others). As early as 1793, the revolutionary idea of a "sovereign people" came up against its own contradictions. This averred universalism suffered a setback as soon as it became necessary to identify a people and decide who would belong to it, over what territory it would exercise its sovereignty, and who would benefit from State subsidies. This process was accompanied by a strong penetration of the State into social life, which took the form of greater administrative and police control. As Gérard Noiriel masterfully teaches us: "since 1789, the intensification of encounters that had resulted from industrialization and urbanization from 1750 onwards have further multiplied the number of individuals who are no longer under the gaze of their group of belonging, and reinforced the social need for objectified identities in the form of passports and various certificates."[31] This evolution did not proceed without resistance, but the Third Republic got the better of the recalcitrants, for as everyone would have to learn, from now on, "A man must have a nationality as he must have a nose and two ears."[32]

The process of national integration is a contract. The viability of the liberal State depends upon its ability to develop its social

---

30 TN: Émile Durkheim, *The Division of Labor in Society*, trans. W. D. Halls (New York: Free Press, 1997). First published in 1893.

31 Gérard Noiriel, *La tyrannie du national: Le droit d'asile en Europe, 1793–1993* (Paris: Calmann-Lévy, 1991), 69.

32 Ernest Gellner, *Nations and Nationalism* (Ithaca, NY: Cornell University Press, 1983), 6. Quoted in ibid., 69.

arm. Thus, national integration would also take the form of social integration, but the social would be subordinated to the national. Most of the social gains of the Third Republic were reserved for "nationals." This was stipulated in the French Nationality Law of 1889, the fruit of long and bitter negotiations between employers and the military, on the one hand, who supported the right of the soil for recruiting workers and soldiers, and the aristocracy, on the other, who supported birthright. To please both sides, the law created a "two-tiered" naturalization system; the result was that foreigners would henceforth require identification. What ensued was a reconfiguration of the labor market based on nationality, and the exclusion of non-nationals (many of them European), who had become foreigners.

The structural bond that united the white working classes—which were becoming more and more white—with the State and the classes that dominate it, became an increasingly tangible reality. In fact, these measures were put in place just a few years after the Paris Commune and at the height of the colonial boom, a few years after the Berlin Conference (1885) that sealed Africa's fate. The slave trade had been abolished, but colonial appetites had not. Western powers carved up the pie shamelessly; they couldn't afford to recognize the fires spreading both at home and abroad, especially as competition between Western nations (and bourgeoisies) was raging. National unity was an economic imperative, but also an imperative of war. It was precisely at this time that the social pact, a corollary of the national pact, took effect in the colonial metropolises in the form of social and political rights. Judge for yourself:

1789: Declaration of the Rights of Man and of the Citizen—France
1825: Recognition of trade unions—Great Britain
1841: Ban on child labor for children under eight—France
1853: Eight-hour working day for women and children—Great Britain
1864: Right to strike—France
1884: Recognition of trade unions—France
1875: Right to strike—Great Britain

1890: Weekly time off on Saturday and Sunday—Great Britain
1906: One day off per week—France
1910: Establishment of the ten-hour workday—France

Noiriel adds:

The nationalization of French society between the 1880s and the First World War led not only to the definition of a new social group made up of citizens with common interests and a shared sense of belonging to the same community, but also to the invention of a new technology for identifying individuals. An instrument essential to a homogeneous, pacified, and centralized political space, this technology became the fundamental means of protecting the interests of the group.[33]

Poulantzas goes one step further: "[C]oncentration camps are a modern invention in the added sense that the frontier-gates close on 'anti-nationals' for whom time and national historicity are in *suspense*."[34] Jews, Gypsies, and all the minorities produced by the nationalization of populations know a thing or two about this. In addition, legislation protecting the national labor market, born during the Third Republic and consolidated in the interwar period and under Vichy, was renewed following Liberation.[35]

However, there is a blind spot in Gérard Noiriel's surgical analysis of the emergence of the nation-state: he underestimates its colonial and imperialist character, which makes it a national *and* a racial State, given that imperialism "is consubstantial with the modern nation in the sense that it cannot be other than *inter*nationalization, or rather *trans*nationalization, of the processes of labour and capital."[36] Sadri Khiari is probably the decolonial theorist to have best brought to light the historical materiality of the racial State:

---

33 Noiriel, *La tyrannie du national*, 170.
34 Poulantzas, *State, Power, Socialism*, 128.
35 Noiriel, *La tyrannie du national*, 137.
36 Poulantzas, *State, Power, Socialism*, 119.

The national social pact is also a *racial* pact. National "Gallic" integration within the space of the French borders was juxtaposed with a national colonial integration around belonging to a statutory "French" group, itself within the context of the larger statutory grouping of white-European civilization. National identity, constructed both in relation to Europe and to colonized peoples, thus blended two types of partly antagonistic identities. The first was specifically *national*, shaped around the myth of an eternal France with supposedly Gallic origins. The second was *transnational*, created around white-European-Christian supremacy of supposedly Greek origins whose first borders were the French territories of the empire. French national identity, which knits the republican pact together and flows through social logics and State politics, is an imperial identity, or, in other words, colonial/racial. The French nation is an *imperial nation*.[37]

At the end of the nineteenth century, racial distinctions were becoming more pronounced. When the nationality law was passed in 1889, French society was already saturated with xenophobia, racism, and the sense of its own superiority. However, the Haitian Revolution unsettled the naturalists' assurances and loudly ushered the enslaved into History, as the victorious resistance restored to the oppressed their full humanity, their capacity to both survive and pose a threat. At the same time, the presence of non-Whites inside the metropolises was becoming increasingly massive. The demand for cheap labor increased, and the proletariat diversified. European and non-white foreigners were now numerous within national spaces, where they competed with national workers. Governmentality becomes properly racial when the indigenous appears in the metropolis—whether as a soldier or as part of the workforce—and threatens racial homogeneity. The risk of heterogeneity reshuffled the deck of social relations and the social pact, whose racial character became more pronounced. It was imperative that white homogeneity be reaffirmed. The State now had to regulate interracial relations,

---

37 Khiari, *The Colonial Counter-Revolution*, 62–3.

as the growing number of citizens increased the number of eligible persons and destabilized the labor market, which had been reserved for nationals. Racism became a cornerstone of social relations, as the French space needed to be protected, if only to ensure the effectiveness of the social/racial pact between the dominant and ruling classes and the white subaltern classes. Like René Gallissot, we have legitimate reasons to doubt that the development of xenophobic nationalism was "a simple perversion of the anger of the masses, for the integration of the working class into the nation-state presupposes a material support," which the notion of "national preference" can translate into priority for employment, housing, etc … .[38] At this point, however, we are still in a national-racial in-between, as non-French Europeans were also victims of these new apparatuses of control. Their subaltern status was maintained until the end of the Second World War and the beginning of the construction of Europe, a new phase in the consolidation of the Western bourgeois bloc as it faced raging anti-colonial revolts. Until this final stage, it was social democracy that set the rules for the new compromise of capital and labor in which race would play a central role.

SOCIAL DEMOCRACY TO THE RESCUE OF THE RACIAL STATE

As previously stated, in the interwar period, Nazi Germany could be considered an anachronism. Western nation-states had undergone a transformation. Under the impetus of their respective bourgeoisies, they adapted to meet the challenges of modernity: conquering and controlling world markets, setting up an interstate system of world governance, and inventing a community of interests between themselves and the white proletariat. To achieve this, they had to agree to change—to soften their conception of race, to shift from the slave system to segregation in the United States, and from genocidal conquest to the civilizing mission in France. Granted, England

---

38 TN: Nadir Boumaza, Ghislaine Clément, and René Gallissot, *Ces migrants qui font le prolétariat* (Paris: Méridiens-Klincksieck, 1994), 257.

and France possessed a veritable "living space" (*Lebensraum*)—the colonial empire Germany had been deprived of by the Treaty of Versailles in 1919, a national humiliation that the Nazis were able to exploit to their advantage. At the end of this climactic fury of unbridled nationalism and racism, Nazism capitulated to its opponents, who were just as racist but less fanatical and much more pragmatic. Indeed, they had to contain communism, whose influence had been unflagging since the Russian Revolution, as well as the anti-colonial revolutions. Enter the historic compromise between capital and labor, between a bourgeoisie on the brink of collapse and a Communist Party that, while triumphant, had failed to seize power. Enter social democracy. 1945 was a pivotal year for a new chapter in the social/racial pact. On May 8, the Republic is reestablished and the rule of law succeeds Vichy, but it commits colonial massacres in Sétif and Guelma in Algeria, killing tens of thousands, in Syria, and later, in Madagascar and Cameroon. All the contradictions of the racial State were crystallized on May 8, 1945. Just as French workers won the right to paid leave in 1936, a "comprehensive social security plan designed to ensure that all citizens have a livelihood in every event that they are unable to secure it through work" proposed by the National Council of the Resistance was adopted in October 1945. The preamble to the Fourth Republic recognized everyone's right to health protection, material security, rest, and leisure. There is no doubt that the class struggle suffered, in the face of a managerial class weakened by five years of loyal and zealous collaboration with the Nazis (major movements for workers' strikes took place, notably in 1947), but the oppression of colonized peoples was not called into question, nor was the privilege of the white working class. Like the Haitian Revolution before them, the Vietnamese and Algerian revolutions unsettled the architecture of the racial State but did not destroy it. De Gaulle would be the strategist of the colonial counter-revolution that absorbed the shock of losing the colonies and maintained France's position as a world power.

The French army's capitulation in 1940 to the external-internal enemy, an enemy external to France and internal to the white world, was a terrible dilemma. So was the French army's defeat by revolts led by the peoples of the empire, that is to say by the internal-external enemy, an enemy internal to French political space and external to the white world. De Gaulle's self-appointed "mission" was to resolve this dilemma.[39]

The result is well known: *Françafrique*, the French bloc in power's response to the challenges posed by struggles for independence.[40] A new stage of globalization was inaugurated: the stage of "structural adjustments." The colossal indebtedness of newly independent countries set them on a disastrous course. To pay its debts, the African continent had to submit to the demands of the IMF and the World Bank, while States had to renounce their sovereignty and public policies and cut back on social spending (for health, for education) to indulge in unbridled liberalism and privatization. A new kind of collaboration emerged. The hegemony of the Western power blocs spread to the Global South through the systematic elimination of revolutionary leaders and socialist projects ([Patrice] Lumumba, [Thomas] Sankara, [Amílcar] Cabral, [Mehdi] Ben Barka, [Félix-Roland] Moumié, and so forth),[41] as well as through

---

39 Khiari, *The Colonial Counter-Revolution*, 68–9.

40 TN: *Françafrique*, a term first evoked by Félix Houphouët-Boigny, president of the Ivory Coast, in the mid-1950s to tout the economic and political benefits of Franco-African collaboration and redeployed by French activist and historian François-Xavier Versachave in 1999 to denounce France's continued neocolonial footprint and covert operations in Africa. See Versachave, *La Françafrique: Le plus long scandale de la République* (Paris: Stock, 1998). For a brief history of the term, see Boubacar Boris Diop, "Françafrique: A Brief History of a Scandalous Word," *NewAfrican Magazine*, March 23, 2018, last accessed June 11, 2024, https://newafricanmagazine.com/16585/.

41 TN: Patrice Lumumba, independence leader (of the Congolese National Movement, MNC) and first prime minister of the Democratic Republic of Congo (June–September 1960), executed in January 1961; Thomas Sankara, military officer, Marxist revolutionary, and Pan-Africanist who served as president of Burkina Faso (from his coup in August 1983 until his assassination in October 1987); Amílcar Cabral, agricultural engineer, nationalist leader, poet, and founder and secretary-general of the African Party for the Independence of Guinea and Cape Verde (PAIGC), killed in 1973; Mehdi Ben Barka, Moroccan head of the left-wing National Union of Popular Forces (UNFP) and secretary of the Tricontinental

the cooption of elites integrated into "happy globalization,"[42] the long arm of the racial/imperial State.

Since then, the bourgeois bloc in France has been steadily regaining power and reestablishing the balance of power it enjoys within the State. The fall of the Berlin Wall in 1989, followed by the collapse of the USSR in 1991, hastened the end of communism as a revolutionary utopia even as big business triumphed.

THE EUROPEAN UNION AS A RACIAL SUPERSTATE

The European Union plays a pivotal role in the strengthening of white Europe throughout the world. Case in point: the change, on September 10, 2019, of the title of "European Commissioner for Migration" to "Commissioner for Protecting our European Way of Life."[43] That's exactly what the project of Europe's construction is all about: a means for European States, seeing their colonies slipping away from them, to find another way of strengthening and securing their hegemonic position around the world. European institutions are merely the concentrated expression of national ruling classes, whose power is partly transferred to a supra-State level. For Hamid Dabashi, Europe has historically formed a "barricade" against the world.[44] The economic and political consolidation of Europe's

---

Conference, disappeared in Paris in 1965; Félix-Roland Moumié, anti-colonialist Cameroonian leader, assassinated in November 1960.

42 TN: "Happy globalization"—a literal translation of the French *mondialisation heureuse*—refers to a late 1990s and early 2000s liberal analysis of globalization as carrying incontrovertible economic and geopolitical benefits. The term first appeared as the title of French businessman and political adviser Alan Minc's book, *La mondialisation heureuse*, published in 1997 by Plon (Paris).

43 TN: The title shifted from Commission on "Migration, Home Affairs, and Citizenship" to "Protecting Our European Way of Life." See, for instance, Jennifer Rankin, "MEPs Damn 'Protecting European Way of Life' Job Title," *Guardian*, September 11, 2019, last accessed June 11, 2024, www.theguardian.com/world/2019/sep/11/meps-damn-insulting-protecting-our-european-way-of-life-job-title.

44 Hamid Dabashi, founder of the Center for Palestine Studies at Columbia University, and author of *Europe and Its Shadows: Coloniality after Empire* (London, Pluto Press, 2019).

nation-states therefore indisputably involves the consolidation of the EU. Identity groups that mobilized behind the slogan "Defend Europe" were not misguided: the defense of whiteness no longer necessarily falls to nation-states alone.[45] As such, the intensification of racism and the far right in the EU does not occur in spite of the EU's policies, but precisely because of them. Moreover, the far right has now perfectly adapted to the EU; it even harbors the hope of gaining a majority position within it (in Sweden, Poland, Hungary, Italy, France perhaps ...). Khiari writes that "the acceleration of European construction is accompanied by an accentuation of racial differentiation, as much within the limits of the European Union and within the borders of the Hexagon."[46]

This point had already been made in the 1980s by René Gallissot, who reminds us that, in the face of decolonization processes and various migrations, national identity had to be accompanied by an identity of a "cultural nature": "the defense of French identity is also a defense of European identity, and it is the logic of civilizational superiority that grants the latter its inherited essence."[47]

The EU does, however, have a political weakness that must be pointed out. While there is indeed a dual process at work in the construction of Europe—on the one hand, the strengthening of "this identity bound around the enclosure as European, white, and Christian"[48] (notably among the section of the population that voted "yes" on the European Constitution), and on the other, the strengthening of French nationalism among a whole section of the population (upon which nationalist supporters of a Frexit rely)—this process is unfolding at the expense of the social pact. While national bourgeoisies had, up until now, succeeded in universalizing their interests

---

45 Formed in the late 1960s around Alain de Benoist, the Groupement de recherche et d'études pour la civilisation européenne (GRECE) [Research and Study Group for European Civilization] has set an example in France and elsewhere in Europe by promoting the idea of a white, Celtic, and Roman European civilization.

46 Khiari, *The Colonial Counter-Revolution*, 220.

47 TN: René Gallissot, "Le racisme n'est pas chez l'autre," *L'homme et la société*, no. 77–78 (1985): 19.

48 TN: Khiari, *The Colonial Counter-Revolution*, 221.

by including the working class in a relatively balanced social/racial pact, the EU no longer grants, within the frame of its rabid competition with emergent capitalist powers, the same advantages to the subaltern classes on a European scale. The EU is technocratic, anti-democratic, and anti-social. In short, it calls into question the overall apparatus of the integral racial State, which also derived its legitimacy from its social arm. In so doing, it shatters the consensus that made the nation-state's fortune, and produces dissent on both the far-left and the far-right ends of the political spectrum, as well as among the classes that have been sacrificed. The State now rests solely upon the racial pact, which clear-sighted rulers fear is wearing thin. Indeed, how can they maintain power and methodically pursue the demolition of the historic compromise between capital and labor that benefited the former, as social unrest directed primarily at the government's liberal policies and the State's institutions is growing?

The answer: racism. And yet, this solution is a double-edged sword that can lean toward a fascist outcome as much as a revolutionary one.

Today, the bourgeois bloc is experiencing a major crisis. The great capitalist powers are engaged in a fierce competition that is as terrifying as it is fatal. For the first time in modern history, the Western bloc is in decline. On the one hand, imperialist wars are ending in crushing defeats, while Africa increasingly slips out of France and the United States' grip to China's benefit in particular. On the other, peoples of the Global South are revolting en masse as they struggle to organize themselves in the absence of utopia. This decline is not without repercussions for the enforcement of the racial pact. The crisis affects the white middle classes, which are seeing their hopes of upward social mobility betrayed. Anger is growing. Indeed, if the global profit rate is falling, Western ruling classes must go elsewhere to round up their margins. Why not go after the very material bases of white privilege, those commonly referred to as "established social rights": labor law and social security, wages, pensions, hospitals, schools, and public services. With ultraliberalism as their last hope, the ruling classes at both the national and the European level are mobilizing. The means to this end: white pride, migrant hunting, and Islamophobia. Is it any wonder, then, that the false injunction to integrate persists pathologically? Are questions like "Is Islam compatible with our values?" not precisely the Republican way of asking whether the indigenous of France, like the indigenous peoples of the Americas, possess a soul?

The spirit of Valladolid lives on in the mind, as it does in the State. If you'll bear with me, you'll see in the next chapter how the forces of the left, and in particular, the French Communist Party, acting as organs of what Gramsci calls "political society," were part and parcel of this process of producing the "integral" racial State.

Race and Political Society

Despite this mistake, the history of the PCF is honorable.[1]

—Communists

It would be tedious to rehearse the history of class collaboration (strongly facilitated by racial solidarity) of all French workers' organizations. I will focus here on the two main organizations, the PCF[2] and the CGT,[3] which are most representative of the relation that ultimately became an organic connection between the political and trade union forces and the imperialist bourgeoisie. I am not unaware that there existed in France a true internationalism both among these organizations and beyond them, but for these purposes, I am more interested in drawing up an inventory of the key moments that strengthened the working class' ties to the racial State, for these fully implicate not only the bourgeois class (as in the previous chapter), but also the most powerful political and trade union leaders of the progressive camp, who thereby contributed to producing the French nation-state and, consequently, its whiteness.

I. The Nationalization of the PCF, or, the Strengthening of Its Ties to the Racial State

The English proletariat is actually becoming more and more bourgeois, so that this most bourgeois of all nations is apparently aiming ultimately at the possession of a bourgeois aristocracy and

---

1 "Des communistes répondent à Michel Onfray" (Communists respond to Michel Onfray), Le Club de Médiapart, August 3, 2022, last accessed June 11, 2024, https://blogs.mediapart.fr/les-communistes/blog/030822/des-communistes-re-pondent-michel-onfray.
2 TN: PCF stands for the Parti communiste français (French Communist Party).
3 TN: CGT stands for the Confédération générale du travail unitaire (General Confederation of Labour).

a bourgeois proletariat *alongside* the bourgeoisie. For a nation which exploits the whole world this is of course to a certain extent justifiable.[4]

... You ask me what the English workers think about colonial policy. Well, exactly the same as they think about politics in general. There is no workers' party here, there are only Conservatives and Liberal-Radicals, and the workers gaily share the feast of England's monopoly of the world market and the colonies.[5]

At the time of writing these first few lines in a letter to Marx dated October 7, 1858, Engels could not have known how his observations about the counter-revolutionary future of political societies in advanced capitalist countries would turn out. And it is unlikely that he could have predicted the colonial fervor and effective power of nationalism, saturated by colonial racism, that would take hold of working-class political formations in imperialist centers. This movement to nationalize the proletariat—which, as we will see, would always prove consistent—can only be understood if we acknowledge the following: That forces with revolutionary potential broke with the relation of rule that bound them to what we could call a "theory of truth." And that capitalism, in its supreme stage—imperialism—generates a regime of structural inequality and injustice on a global scale. The progressive abandonment of this truth could not be achieved without the strategic activity of the ruling classes within the State or the agreement of its standing political forces. If the "history of the working class is the history of its struggles against the bourgeoisie,"[6] it is also the history of the proletariat's identification with the nation-state, within which a power relation that was *also* a class relation was crystallized. To be sure, the bourgeoisie largely dominates this power relation; yet, however

---

4   TN: Friedrich Engels, Letter to Karl Marx (October 7, 1858), last accessed June 11, 2024, www.marxists.org/archive/lenin/works/1916/oct/x01.htm.
5   TN: Friedrich Engels, Letter to Karl Marx (September 12, 1882), last accessed June 11, 2024, www.marxists.org/archive/lenin/works/1916/oct/x01.htm.
6   Nicos Poulantzas, *State, Power, Socialism* (London: Verso, 2014 [1978]), 130.

dominated, the organized proletariat struggles to leave its mark on the State on a social level as well as on a national/racial level. In the pages that follow, I will consider the history of this power struggle and of the abandonment of the authority of Truth—meant to orient revolutionary action—through the acceptance of a deal that gave birth to a French "people" (formally) emancipated of its class contradictions yet steeped in racial ones.

THE RIF AND THE ÉTOILE NORD-AFRICAINE

On rare occasions throughout its history, the PCF was able to free itself from the jaws of the racial State.

For this, we have to thank the Russian Revolution of 1917, which sent such shockwaves across French worker organizations that they adopted internationalist positions at odds with their chauvinistic inclinations. The Third International, founded in March 1919 in Moscow, established twenty-one terms of admission for new parties. The eighth condition is of particular interest:

> Parties in countries whose bourgeoisie possess colonies and oppress other nations must pursue a most well-defined and clear-cut policy in respect of colonies and oppressed nations. Any part wishing to join the Third International must ruthlessly expose the colonial machinations of the imperialists of its "own" country, must support—in deed, not merely in word—every colonial liberation movement, demand the expulsion of its compatriot imperialists from the colonies, inculcate in the hearts of the workers of its own country an attitude of true brotherhood with the working population of the colonies and the oppressed nations, and conduct systematic agitation among the armed forces against all oppression of the colonial peoples.[7]

---

7   TN: "Terms of Admission into Communist International" [July 1920], first published in *The Second Congress of the Communist International, Verbatim Report* (Petrograd: Communist International, 1921). Published in V. I. Lenin, *Collected Works*, trans. Julius Katzer, vol. 31, 4th edn (Moscow: Progress Publishers, 1965),

The PCF was founded on the basis of these twenty-one terms in 1920 at the Tours Congress. The French Communist movement experienced its "heroic"[8] decade on the heels of this congress. Historians have all noted the crucial role of the Third International, whose constant and occasionally direct application of pressure was decisive in stimulating internationalist agendas. Yet, these "heroic" acts marking the history of the PCF "in deeds not words" can be counted on two fingers of a single hand: the struggle against the colonial Rif War, and with more ambiguous commitment, the creation of the Étoile Nord-Africaine.

The struggle against the Rif War was likely the only time the Communist Party engaged in real anti-imperialist propaganda campaigns among the working class through marches and strikes, as well as within the army. In Morocco, the PCF openly supported Abd el-Krim. The CGTU[9] called for a strike "against the Franco-Rif war and against our government, which is responsible for it." This political strike brought together 900,000 workers on October 12, 1925. There was considerable repression. In addition, over 1,000 insubordinate soldiers were tried before military tribunals.[10] A March 1923 appeal by the Jeunesse Communiste[11] set the tone: "Young worker! The tricolor flag, which once signified the freedom of the people, today is the symbol of their subjection. Under no circumstances will you accept the humiliating role of counter-revolutionary agent."[12] Clandestine communist newspapers distributed in the barracks declared: "Soldiers of France and Spain, fraternize with Abd el-Krim."

206–11, last accessed June 11, 2024, www.marxists.org/archive/lenin/works/1920/jul/x01.htm.

8   Alain Ruscio, *Les communistes et l'Algérie, des origines à la guerre d'indépendance, 1920–1962* (Paris: La Découverte, 2019).

9   TN: CGTU stands for Confédération générale du travail unitaire (United General Confederation of Labour).

10   René Dazy, *La partie et le tout: Le P.C.F. et la guerre franco-algérienne* (Paris: Syllepse, 1990), 31.

11   TN: Jeunesse Communiste (JC), or Communist Youth Movement, renamed the Mouvement jeunes communistes de France (MJCF) in 1956.

12   Fédération Nationale des Jeunesses Communistes, "Manifeste aux Conscrits," *L'Humanité*, March 11, 1923, n.p.

The Fourth Congress of the PCF was held in Clichy amid anti-colonial mobilization against the Rif War. It is perhaps the only congress at which an internationalist position was clearly asserted, as is evident from an article written by the Algerian communist militant El Djazairi, published on the eve of the congress and entitled "Le Parti communiste et la question coloniale" [The Communist Party and the colonial question]. The article posed the problem as follows:

> It would be a mistake to believe that we must wait for the Communist Revolution in Europe to liberate the mass of colonial peoples from the yoke of imperialism. These peoples, who are odiously exploited, want nothing more than to drive the invader away immediately.[13]

The Third International's position was very clear: Communist parties had to be formed autonomously in the colonies. But the PCF leadership was very reluctant. It was not until 1936 that the Algerian Communist Party[14] was founded. Many Algerian communists, however, were eager to organize the struggle for independence in Algeria. The PCF took the initiative of assembling them into a dedicated organization, the Étoile Nord-Africaine (ENA),[15] which played a considerable role in the development of the national movement in Algeria in the 1920s and 1930s.[16] The ENA was founded in Paris in 1924.[17]

---

13 *Cahiers du bolchévisme*, no. 7 (January 2, 1925). Cited in Jacques Jurquet, *La révolution nationale algérienne et le Parti communiste français*, vol. 2, *1920–1939* (Paris: Éditions du centenaire, 1974), 254. Jurquet's five-volume study contains many facts about and analyses of the period dating from 1847 to 1962. His reading is indispensable to understanding, among other things, the power of social and national movements in Algeria at the turn of the twentieth century, as well as the PCF's inability to grasp their reach.

14 TN: Parti communiste algérien (PCA).

15 TN: North-African Star.

16 The print run of the organization's newspaper, *Glorieuse Étoile Nord-Africaine, El Oumma*, increased from 12,000 in 1932 to 44,000 in 1934. See Jurquet, *La révolution nationale algérienne*, 304.

17 During the Premier Congrès des travailleurs nord-africains [First Congress of North African Workers] on December 7, 1924. Some historians have put forward a later date: 1926. See Jurquet, *La révolution nationale algérienne*, 241ff.

In the 1920s, at each of its congresses, the Communist International reaffirmed the need to create independent Communist parties in the colonies. This was the case in Vietnam, where the Party was founded in 1930 completely independently from the French Party. But not in Algeria.

The relationship between the Étoile Nord-Africaine and the Party was far from simple. The PCF was anxious to control the ENA and did not regard it as embryonic of an autonomous party. For their part, ENA leaders felt that the Party's leadership was placing national demands on the back burner, and they sought the ENA's independence from the PCF. In 1936 the PCF reluctantly agreed to the creation of the Algerian Communist Party, over which it persistently tried to exercise control.[18] This marked the end of the PCF's "heroic decade."

Although the PCF disseminated anti-colonial propaganda in the 1920s, it never developed a firm, consistent strategy in this area. It never fully stood by the policy required of the eighth condition or did so only under pressure from the Third International. Even in its early, most internationalist years, the Party never consistently organized anti-colonial propaganda campaigns among the working class, as was required by the eighth condition. The PCF's position toward the Étoile Nord-Africaine, from its creation in 1926 to its dissolution by the Front Populaire government in 1937 (sanctioned by the PCF), is emblematic of the transition from the (albeit limited) internationalism of the 1920s to the chauvinism of the 1930s and beyond.

WHEN YOU CAN'T SEE THE FOREST FOR THE TREES

Before identifying the various types of colonial racism, it's worth noting that there have always been genuine internationalists within the Communist Party who sought to put into practice the Marxist

---

18 On the complex relationship between the PCF and the PCA, and on the latter's activities, see Ruscio, *Les communistes et l'Algérie*, as well as Jacques Jurquet's five-volume work, cited above. As for the Étoile Nord-Africaine, it was dissolved by the Front Populaire government in January 1937.

slogan "proletarians of all countries, nations, and oppressed peoples, unite." In the early years of the Party's existence, the fight for social emancipation in metropolitan France could be connected to the struggle against colonialism and imperialism, in particular through *concrete unity* with nationalist movements in the colonies. But this trend only manifested early on, and later opportunities would never again be seized. Nevertheless, some communist militants continued to work in this spirit through short-lived actions, which led to their isolation, and even their exclusion from the Party.

Let's cite a few names, for the record. Those of French Algerian communists who joined the FLN,[19] like Fernand Iveton, who was taken to the guillotine on February 11, 1957, along with two other Algerians, Mohamed Lakhnèche and Mohamed Ouenouri—one of whom said to him before he died: "Iveton, my brother." And the officer-candidate Henri Maillot, who deserted in April 1956 by hijacking a truck full of weapons and ammunition to join a communist guerilla[20] in the region of Orléansville—and was murdered by French soldiers on June 5, 1956. And Maurice Laban, a former member of the International Brigades, who was murdered with Maillot.[21] And Raymonde Peschard, a member of the ALN,[22] killed in combat on November 26, 1957, and recognized as a "shaheed"[23] by Algeria. There were so many others. We should also mention the communists who later joined or organized networks in France to help the FLN, such as Henri Curiel, Jean-Louis Hurst, and Louis Ohrant. And Maurice Lurot, the communist and CGT member, who was assassinated on July 14, 1953, during a demonstration at the Place de la Nation. For several years, Lurot had co-organized the procession of Algerian workers in trade union demonstrations. The July 14th march ended in police machine-gun fire: six patriotic Algerian

---

19   TN: Front de Libération Nationale (National Liberation Front).
20   These guerrillas [*maquis*] were later integrated into the FLN.
21   Alongside their brothers Abdelkader Zelmatt, Djilali Moussaoui, and Belkacem Hannoun. Their five bodies were dragged by military trucks to the village of Lamartine, where they were buried somewhere outside of the cemetery.
22   TN: Armée de libération nationale (Algerian National Liberation Army).
23   TN: Arabic for martyr.

workers were killed alongside Lurot, and dozens more wounded.[24] There were also the dockworkers who refused to load weapons en route to Vietnam in the 1950s, and their descendants who did the same during the war against Iraq in 1991. There were the "white soldiers of Hô Chi Minh," the French soldiers who joined the ranks of the Việt Minh[25]; the sailor Henri Martin, who was imprisoned for inciting insubordination among his comrades deployed to Vietnam; Raymond Dien, sentenced in 1950 for blocking a train of armored vehicles destined for Vietnam; and Georges Boudarel, a communist civil servant in Hanoi, who joined the Việt Minh in 1950.[26]

The memory of these militants should be honored today and their actions held up as exemplary to show that an alternative to the alliance with the imperialist bourgeoisie was possible. This brings us to the heart of the matter.

FROM PROUDHON TO THOREZ, COLONIAL RACISM'S ROOTS IN THE FRENCH WORKERS' MOVEMENT

Chauvinism has been temporarily thwarted at times, but in the end, it has always imposed itself, from Proudhon to Thorez, by way of Jules Guesde.

In the nineteenth century, the workers' movement was initially under the influence of Proudhonism, a movement Marxists vehemently fought against. In writing *The Poverty of Philosophy* in 1847

---

24 Abdelkader Draris, Mouhoub Illoul, Amar Tadjadit, Larbi Daoui, Tahar Magdène, and Abdallah Bacha. A plaque was installed at Place de la Nation to commemorate them ... in 2017. A few days after their murders, their bodies were displayed alongside Lurot's at the Maison des Métallos, where tens of thousands of Parisians came to pay tribute to them. The red flag and the flag of Algerian resistance were brandished together. See Daniel Kupferstein's documentary film, *Les Balles du 14 juillet 1953* (The Bullets of July 14, 1953), 2014.

25 See Jaques Doyon, *Les soldats blancs de Hô Chi Minh* (Verviers: Marabout, 1986 [1973]).

26 The "Boudarel Affair" broke in 1991: a campaign led against the then-professor at the Université Paris VII Jussieu accused him of having tortured French prisoners-of-war in a Việt Minh reeducation camp, where he served as political commissioner. See his autobiography, *Autobiographie*, published by Jacques Bertoin, Paris, in 1991.

(a response to Proudhon's book, *Philosophy of Poverty*), Marx liquidated Proudhonism on a theoretical level, but not on a political one.
Engels was perhaps overly optimistic when he wrote:

> The Commune was also the grave of the Proudhon school of
> socialism. Today this school has vanished from French working
> class circles; among them now ... Marx's theory rules unchal-
> lenged. Only among the "radical" bourgeoisie are there still
> Proudhonists.[27]

Subsequent events proved him wrong.

In short, Proudhonism reflects the petit-bourgeois utopia that
consists in wanting to erase the flaws of capitalism without confronting the pillar on which the system rests—private ownership of
the means of production. Proudhon finds the *good* side and the *bad*
side of every aspect of capitalism, neutralizing the bad side without
destroying it by using a peaceable method that does not involve
class struggle and strikes a balance with the "good side." This is the
Proudhonian dialectic.[28]

This appetite for balance and moderation, this pacifism, this rejection of the necessarily violent nature of revolution, have recently
struck a chord for a certain Michel Onfray, who intends to rehabilitate Proudhon against Marx.[29] To Onfray, Proudhon is a man of the
soil, a real French plebe, whereas Marx, born of a converted Jewish
father and a Dutch mother, and married to a German aristocrat,
cannot legitimately represent the people. Already in 1911, the far
right had seized on this figure by creating the Cercle Proudhon,[30]

---

27 Frederick Engels, introduction to Karl Marx, *The Civil War in France*, London,
March 18, 1891 (on the twentieth anniversary of the Paris Commune), last accessed
June 11, 2024, www.marxists.org/archive/marx/works/1871/civil-war-france/
postscript.htm.

28 Proudhon's knowledge of how to utilize the "good side" of a situation eventually
led him to cozy up to the government of Napoleon III.

29 See Romaric Godin, "Onfray, un proudhonisme de droite?" *Mediapart*, June
18, 2020, www.mediapart.fr/journal/france/180620/onfray-un-proudhonisme-de-
droite.

30 TN: The Proudhon Circle, a proto-fascist, national syndicalist political group
founded in 1911 by disciples of Georges Sorel, Georges Valois, and Édouard Berth.

which issued from the ranks of Charles Maurras's Action Française.[31] According to historian Zeev Sternhell, the Cercle Proudhon was the founding nucleus of fascist ideology in France.[32]

In line with the most widespread ideas of his time, Proudhon upheld the theory of racial inequality; the superiority of the white race could be easily proven ... by the fact that it dominated other races.

Like most nineteenth-century French socialists, Proudhon was in favor of colonization, which was justified by the superiority of French civilization and could only carry benefits for the "backward peoples." Some socialists dressed up this supremacism with utopian aims: the colony was seen as a virgin land in which new forms of social organization could be tested out. A sort of kibbutz ideology *avant la lettre* ...

From the very beginnings of colonization, the notion that the salvation of colonial peoples *depended* on the fate of the revolutionary movement in metropolitan France was already well established. A colonized people is always *passive*, and must respect the agenda of the *active* people of the colonial metropole. The idea that the future of colonial emancipation lay in the metropole dominates the entire history of the French worker and Communist movements. Jaurès picked up this refrain when he proposed a trade-off that could not have been more unequal: France would contribute its culture ... and Algeria its agriculture. There was something to gain for everyone, though of course, generosity was on the French side since, as he stated in Albi in 1884: "Our colonies will become French in heart and mind only when they understand some French."[33]

---

31 TN: Action Française (French Action), a French far-right monarchist movement founded by Maurice Pujo and Henri Vaugeois in 1899 in response to left-wing intellectuals' interventions on behalf of Alfred Dreyfus.

32 Zeev Sternhell, *La droite révolutionnaire 1885–1914: Les origines françaises du fascisme* (Paris: Seuil, 1978), 391–6.

33 TN: Jean Jaurès, *L'Alliance française, association nationale pour la propagande de la langue française dans les colonies et à l'étranger* (Albi, 1884). Partial translation in Janet Horne, "'To Spread the French Language Is to Extend the *Patrie*': The Colonial Mission of the Alliance Française," *French Historical Studies* 40, no. 1 (February 2017): 114.

Among the General Council of the International, the "Proud-honist clique" in Paris tirelessly defended the idea that the peoples of Europe owed their emancipation to the advances of the revolution in France.[34] These peoples were asked to be patient and wait until the French were ready for social revolution, so that they could follow their example.

Another major and equally persistent feature of the chauvinist tendency was its inability to grasp the *political* significance of national revolution and the nationalism of oppressed peoples. Proudhon did not understand national emancipation, which he rejected in the name of social revolution. We can all see how this incapacity has persisted in the movement. In 1916, Lenin referred to it as Proudhonism.[35]

The "Proudhonists" (and Rosa Luxemburg, with whom Lenin had heated debates) held a mechanistic view of the relationship between politics and economics, hence Lenin's writing on "imperialist Economism." They refused to see that the liberation of oppressed nations presupposed a dual transformation within the political arena: on the one hand, the full legal equality of nations; on the other, freedom of *political separation*.[36]

This mechanistic reasoning, this "imperialist Economism," was according to Lenin, "like the old Economics of the years 1894–1902, which argued: capitalism is victorious, *therefore* political questions are a waste of time! Imperialism is victorious, *therefore* political questions are a waste of time!"[37]

We will see how this inability to grasp the political and revolutionary significance of the nationalism of oppressed peoples led the

---

34 Socialists were more preoccupied with the fate of oppressed nations in Europe than with the colonies—this was a defining feature of the Second International.

35 For instance, in "The Discussion on Self-Determination Summed up," Vladimir Lenin writes: "*In the name* of their doctrinaire concept of social revolution, the Proudhonists ignored the international role of Poland and brushed aside national movements." See Lenin, "The Discussion on Self-Determination Summed up" (July 1916), last accessed June 11, 2024, www.marxists.org/archive/lenin/works/1916/jul/x01.htm.

36 Lenin, ibid. TN: Bouteldja adds the term "legal" to Lenin's quote.

37 Ibid.

PCF to oppose the emancipation of French colonies. Nevertheless, with the benefit of hindsight and despite his political clairvoyance, we can't issue Lenin a certificate of absolute decoloniality, given that his defense of the self-determination of oppressed peoples was conditional on their conforming to the interests of the international proletariat. This position, which presupposes the existence of an "actually existing" international proletariat, all parts of which would "simultaneously" experience capitalist oppression as class struggle, is a dead end. This tropism would remain decisive throughout the history of the white left, be it revolutionary or reformist. As Khiari writes:

> Make no mistake, this chauvinism is not antithetical to internationalism, it is in fact—to this day—its dominant form. Imperialism is the export of social, political, and cultural relations. It is also an export of the modalities—the form and substance—of resistance to these social, political and cultural relations.[38]

FRENCH MARXISTS ATTEMPT, IN VAIN, TO FREE THEMSELVES FROM PROUDHONISM

The failure of the French and European workers' movement at the turn of the twentieth century is an important case study for two reasons. It is then that opportunism and social nationalism became inextricably linked, and that the chauvinist tendency, unable to grasp the relationship between the national question and the colonial question, imposed itself.

The end of the nineteenth century saw the rallying of monarchist and clerical parties to the Republic and its "values," including secularism. It could be said that *Republicanism* was born at this moment from a kind of sacred union between the traditional right and the non-Marxist left. "We have saved the Republic," declared Jaurès at the International Socialist Congress in Amsterdam on August 21, 1904.

---

38   Sadri Khiari, *Pour une politique de la racaille: Immigré.e.s, indigènes et jeunes de banlieues* (Paris: Textuel, 2006), 78.

From then on, *Republicanism* and *secularism* spread throughout the French workers' movement, despite the efforts of Marxists. Presenting the Republican configuration of the State as a supreme value is one way to strip it of any class character, and to endow it with positive traits that await only their activation within a linear, progressive vision of revolution.

Jaurès and the reformists occasionally adopted an anti-colonial rhetoric and protested against certain expeditions, such as the 1907 expedition to Morocco. Proudhon himself, at the end of his life, lamented Bugeaud's excesses in Algeria. But they remained committed to the concept of an enlightened imperialism, denouncing the "excesses" of colonialism and defending the idea that colonization could be peaceful and benevolent. As a result, no propaganda was developed to unite the proletariat in France with the oppressed peoples in the colonies.

Jaurès's understanding that capitalism inherently provokes war and his fight against militarism are well known, but he remained uncertain about the course of action to take, especially when he wanted socialists to support "defensive warfare." After his assassination, this confusion persisted among his comrades, leading them to take part in the imperialist war of 1914.

The revolutionary Marxist tendency embodied by Jules Guesde and Paul Lafargue had the merit of having "been successful in sowing the seeds of Marxism and watching them take hold within petty-bourgeois, Proudhonian, pacifist, and chauvinist France."[39]

The years 1880 to 1894 were their best years. Guesde and his comrades fought the colonial policies of French imperialism, notably in the expeditions to Tunisia, Tonkin, Madagascar, and the Congo. But all this remained embryonic, precarious; the emergence of imperialism was not understood. When the Socialist Party (SFIO) was formed in 1905, the Guesdist movement took a hit and Jauresian reformism won out without difficulty.

---

39 According to André Ferrat, *Histoire du Parti Communist français* (Paris: Bureau d'éditions, 1931), republished in 1931 by Éditions Gît-le-coeur (Paris), 34.

WHO WILL DARE SAY: "THE MAIN ENEMY IS IN YOUR OWN COUNTRY"?[40]

In 1907–14, as it was disintegrating, the Guesdist movement failed to grasp the importance of anti-war propaganda; it confined itself to a general and abstract discourse against the capitalist system, without attempting to build a real anti-war movement.

The feelings of workers were naturally colored by pacifism and illusions about the nature of imperialism: a considerable effort at education and propaganda was required, which the labor and Communist movements in France never really attempted. The Guesdists eventually adopted Jaurès's theory according to which it was possible to support a war in certain cases, for instance, when it was "defensive" or when it was a matter of "defending the most socialist country against the least socialist" (by which they meant that France was "more socialist" than Germany). In 1914, nearly all the socialist leaders of the Second International succumbed to collaborating with "their own" imperialist bourgeoisie by voting for war bonds and later participating in the Union Sacrée[41] governments to lead the war. However, within the internationalist camp itself, a dispute arose between proponents of a certain kind of pacifism and those who, like Lenin, sought to transform the imperialist war into a civil war against the bourgeoisie. "The main enemy is in your own country," proclaimed the internationalists.[42]

Lenin understood the full significance of this betrayal by the leaders of the Second International, who had pitted workers against each other in a war fomented by capital's desire to complete the

---

40 Karl Liebknecht, German communist assassinated in Berlin in 1919. TN: Karl Liebnecht, "The Main Enemy Is in Your Own Country!" (leaflet, May 1915), *Socialist Appeal* 3, no. 21 (April 4, 1939): 3, last accessed June 11, 2024, www.marxists.org/history/etol/newspape/themilitant/socialist-appeal-1939/v03n21/liebknecht.htm.

41 TN: The Union Sacrée (Sacred Union) was a political truce in France through which left-wing parties agreed, during the First World War, not to oppose the government or call any strikes.

42 This debate animated the two international Communist conferences in Zimmerwald in September 1915 and Kienthal in April 1916.

division of the world. He understood that this "sacred union" was steeped in a fundamentally reformist and opportunist position, the root cause of which he described as such: in the age of imperialism, part of the proletariat may find it in their interest to support "their own" bourgeoisie, which has promised them some of the crumbs of the planet's plundered riches. Trade union and political leaders of the workers' movement were especially affected by this corruption, which dragged them into class collaboration all the more easily because anti-imperialist revolutionary elements remained scattered and unorganized.

The fate of the Second International teaches us another very important lesson. The socialist leaders who assembled the Union Sacrée were not interested in understanding the nature of imperialism, nor did they seek to grasp the connection between the national question and the colonial question. For them, the "national question" was limited to the fate of Europe's "civilized" nationalities—the Polish, Hungarian, Irish, Serbian, and so on. A wall separated White and Black people, the "civilized" and the "uncivilized," Europe and the rest of the world. Lenin and the Bolsheviks can be credited with having, at least initially, torn down this wall, because they understood that imperialism represents the stage in which the division of all the world's territories among the largest capitalist countries has been completed, and in which maximum profit comes from the systematic enslavement and plunder of the peoples of other countries through war and the militarization of the economy.

THOREZ AND THE IMPLEMENTATION
OF THE RACIAL/COLONIAL DOCTRINE

In May 1936, the Front Populaire government came to power. This shift put an end to anti-colonialism within the PCF.[43] The Communist International's League Against Imperialism disappeared in 1935, leaving the Front Populaire—which also called itself the "national front"—room to maneuver. [René] Gallissot explains:

---

43 See Claude Liauzu, *Aux origines des tiers-mondismes: Colonisés et anticolonialistes en France (1919–1939)* (Paris: L'Harmattan, 1982).

It is through "national State socialization" that the shift from an initially negative integration involving the direct and subversive action of workers, to integration under a social bond through national-nationalist belonging occurs—a shift that Emile Durkheim, specifically, has theorized. The "social bond" must take precedence over class struggles in the form of the nation's "desire to live together," as Renan writes, and this not without the anti-German and colonial patriotism exalted by E. Lavisse ("you will be a soldier, my son"). The Sacred Union of 1914 overcame the confrontations of the Dreyfus Affair. The majority of the SFIO swung toward patriotism, and left-wing Republicanism redoubled its patriotism.[44]

In 1936, Thorez and other leaders of the PCF drew up a detailed doctrine for a characteristically French nationalism, which would dominate the Party's strategy from that point on and expand unfettered when Communist ministers participated in the government at Liberation, from April 1944 until May 1947. The category "class" gradually disappeared, to be replaced by the category "people." One of the major features of this doctrine, the foundations of which can be traced back to the 1920s, had to do with the idea of France's supremacy: Thorez was convinced of the superiority of the French people, of French democracy, and of the French Republic— in short, of "French civilization," to which the peoples of the colonies had *better* adhere. Unable to achieve emancipation on their own, they would have to wait for the proletariat in metropolitan France to enact "its own" social revolution. But what would they be waiting for? Independence? No, because once socialism had been established in Paris, colonial peoples would have no choice but to unite with revolutionary France. National/racial ideology thus turned the internationalist program on its head: independence

---

44   René Gallissot, "Génération algérienne: entretien avec René Gallissot," *Période*, March 28, 2016, last accessed June 11, 2024, http://revueperiode.net/generation-algerienne-entretien-avec-rene-gallissot/. TN: See Emile Durkheim, *The Division of Labour in Society* (1893), trans. W. D. Halls (New York: Free Press, 1997); Ernest Renan, "Qu'est-ce qu'une nation?" lecture, La Sorbonne, Paris, March 11, 1882, in Renan, *Qu'est-ce qu'une nation?* (Paris: Presses-Pocket, 1992).

became counter-revolutionary since it separated the colony from its savior, the proletariat of the metropole. From then on, separatists were stigmatized as enemies of progress, democracy, and revolution.

The explicit rejection of the demand for independence was theorized at this point, in the late 1930s. Robert Deloche, a member of the Colonial Section [of the PCF], wrote in the *Cahiers du bolchévisme* on May 20, 1937:

> Those who, having understood or wanted to understand nothing of the political situation in France and in the world, would like to see colonial peoples rise up today in a violent struggle against French democracy on the pretext of independence, are in reality working toward the victory of fascism and the reinforcement of the enslavement of colonial peoples.[45]

The same year, Thorez asserted that "the interest of the colonial peoples lies *in their unity* with the French people." And he added, in the same spirit as when he extolled French greatness in 1945 that this "free" union of colonial peoples with France would work toward the fulfillment of France's mission in the world.[46]

Another theme emerged at this time, which would be taken up again later on: "colonization with a human face." The critique of colonial oppression aimed to demonstrate that the massacres perpetrated by settlers or the army formed an obstacle to unity with the metropole, which remained the objective. "Self-centered colonization" must be brought to an end as it only prevents unity and harms the "French presence." Similarly, in 1937, Gabriel Péri first evoked the notion that the colonial question must remain "a subordinated part of a larger whole."[47]

---

45   TN: Robert Deloche, "Le Pain, la Paix, la Liberté aux Peuples coloniaux," *Cahiers du bolchévisme*, no. 4–5 (May 20, 1937): 112.

46   Maurice Thorez, "In Order to Go Forward," in *France of the People's Front and Its Mission in the World* (New York: Workers Library Publishers, 1938), 99. From a speech given at the French Communist Party (PCF)'s IX Congress in Arles, December 25, 1937.

47   TN: Gabriel Péri, quoted in Claude Liauzu, *Histoire de l'anticolonialisme en France du XVIe siècle à nos jours* (Paris: Colin, 2007), 176. Translation in

Later on, we will see how this now-classic theme—which distorts a line from Lenin[48]—was reprised to justify the 1956 vote granting the government special powers, allowing Guy Mollet to launch the Algerian War. The affirmation of this relation of subordination has been a constant since the 1930s, whether in geostrategic terms (the colony must remain united with France), political terms (the national struggle depends on the battles waged in metropolitan France), or organizational terms (the PAC must remain subservient to the PCF). Even today, the left has great difficulty accepting the autonomous organization of immigrants and their descendants and has revealed itself incapable of devising an anti-imperialist political strategy.

Thorez's theory on Algeria—a "nation in formation" that should continue to live under French tutelage—is well known. He presented it in a speech in Algiers on February 11, 1939, outlining the reasons for Algeria's incapacity and offering the final word on French chauvinism:

Christopher L. Miller, "The (Revised) Birth of Negritude: Communist Revolution and the 'Immanent Negro' in 1935," *PMLA* 125, no. 3 (May 2010): 744.

48   Another reference to Lenin served as a pretext for Thorez to indicate as clearly as possible that the affirmation of the "right to independence" must not be followed by action: the "right to divorce" is not the obligation to divorce. The use of Lenin's quotation on "freedom to unite" was once again fraudulent. Lenin raised this point at a Party conference in May 1917, in the midst of revolutionary ferment, at a time when the Russian proletariat was preparing to take power. Polish Communists ("Social Democrats" at the time) questioned the wisdom of emphasizing *secession* from the Russian oppressor, when an *alliance* with the Russian workers in proximity to power could be advantageous. Lenin's position was very clear: it is the *right* of Social Democrats to assert the freedom to unite, but it is the *duty* of the Russians to support the right to secession of oppressed nations. While Thorez speaks from the point of view of both the oppressed and the oppressor (preserving only the interests of the latter), Lenin takes on his responsibility as a militant internationalist in the Great Russian chauvinist State, which oppressed more nationalities than any other State, and inflicted the worst damage on Poland ("No one has oppressed the Poles more than the Russian people"). The Communists of the *oppressing nation* must emphasize the freedom of secession, and not the freedom to unite, which is *only one* of the possible positions the oppressed nation might take. TN: Lenin, "Speech on the National Question, April 29 (May 12)," The Seventh (April) All-Russia Conference of the R.S.D.L.P. (B.), April 24–29, 1917, last accessed June 11, 2024, www.marxists.org/archive/lenin/works/1917/7thconf/29d.htm.

There is the Algerian nation, which is being constituted histori-cally and whose evolution can be facilitated and aided by the efforts of the French Republic ... There is the Algerian nation, which is being constituted through the mixture of twenty races. And whoever attempts not to unite, but to try to divide and set all these men against each other today, on the pretext that they are of different religion, race, and color, is acting criminally toward the French motherland, toward our duty to humanity, and toward the people.[49]

Thus, to grow and become a nation, Algeria needed the French Republic and "French democracy." But there is also a second argument: that hastening this process of "birthing a nation" would cause division. So be patient, Algerian comrades, and count on "French democracy" ... which, in February 1939, had only a few months left to live!

The idea that France was a more advanced country than its colonies definitively shaped the PCF's strategy in the 1930s. The Party supported the "politics of French greatness."[50] The tricolor flag—which had been described fifteen years prior as a "symbol of the subjugation of the people"—was brandished with pride. Joan of Arc was celebrated as the "daughter of the people" (a reference to Thorez's autobiography, *Son of the People*). The phrase applied to Algeria, "nation in formation," had not been formulated by chance. It would guide the Party leaders' paternalistic and colonialist practice, as demonstrated by this statement by Léon Feix, a member of the Political Bureau, after the Algerian uprising of November 1954 (which the PCF condemned):

[Algeria] is a nation in formation .... This definition constitutes a decisive contribution by the General Secretary of the French

---

49   TN: Maurice Thorez, "Le Peuple algérien uni autour de la France," speech, February 11, 1939, Algiers, published in *La Brochure populaire*, no. 7 (Paris: April 1939): 12.
50   This is the title of one of Thorez's books, which collects speeches given between 1936 and 1945. The book was published by Éditions Sociales in 1945.

Communist Party to the cause of the liberation of the Algerian people. For the first time, the Algerian question is posed on its own terms.[51]

A SINGLE SOLUTION, THE FRENCH UNION

At Liberation, the PCF participated in the government from 1944 to 1947, yet it completely and openly rallied to the cause of the French colonial/racial State. This strategy, shared by other parties in Western countries, caused immense damage in France and elsewhere, preventing the powerful alliance that could have been forged between the burgeoning postwar struggles for national liberation and the workers' movement in capitalist countries.

At the end of the war, imperialist France sought to regain its position on the international stage. Most of the right-wing political class, and many SFIO politicians, had collaborated with the Nazis; it was up to de Gaulle's team to restore France's power. Among other things, de Gaulle had to contend with the renewed appetites of Great Britain, and the immense ambitions of the United States, which was assuming the leadership of the Western world. Apart from a few small territories, the United States had no colonies: consequently, it tried to enter old Europe's (France and Great Britain), while pretending to support the peoples' just demands for freedom and independence. The leaders of the PCF used this argument again and again to reject any emancipation movement in the colonies, in which they detected the involvement of the United States or Great Britain. During the war, the colonies represented a decisive asset for providing territorial substance to de Gaulle's "Free France," which would otherwise have been reduced to the Carlton Gardens building

---

51   Léon Feix, "Les communistes et la lutte nationale du peuple algérien," *Cahiers du communisme*, no. 2 (February 1955), 156–57, cited by René Dazy, *La partie et le tout: Le P.C.F. et la guerre franco-algérienne* (Paris: Syllepse, 1990), 25. Dazy situates the last mention of this "theory" in a speech by Étienne Fajon dating from February 1957. Two days later, February 14, Thorez concluded: "And now, in accordance with History ... we have modified our formula and rightly speak of the Algerian fact, of a fully formed Algerian nation" (26). The heroic struggle of the Algerian insurgents won out over Thorez's "theory"!

in London ... In late 1942, nearly all of the French Empire (with the exception of Indochina) was called upon to support the Allies and supply troops, in the hundreds of thousands, to Free France. The French Committee of National Liberation (CFLN), which the PCF joined in 1944, was based in Algiers, where it was founded in 1943.

The PCF's *active* support of the French State's imperialist policies dates back to this period.

Florimond Bonte's (the PCF representative for the CFLN) 1943 speech in Algiers attests to this:

> Who better than our present-day colonizers—descendants of those generations that died fighting the battle against material and spiritual ignorance—to feel deeply in their hearts and minds, as an inescapable and fruitful necessity, the solidarity of fates that unites, across oceans, overseas France and metropolitan France?[52]

In early 1944, the CFLN organized the famous Brazzaville Conference, where de Gaulle, faced with the United States' "anti-colonialist" assaults, was called upon to ensure the empire's survival, all the while making a few concessions (the Code de l'Indigénat[53] was abolished, for example). The underlying principles of this conference (in which no representative of the colonized populations took part) were clear: "The ends of the civilizing work accomplished by France in the colonies excludes any idea of autonomy, all possibility of evolution outside the French bloc of the Empire; the constitution of self-governments in the colonies, even in the distant future, is denied."[54] The PCF supported the redressing of the French colonial empire from start to finish.

---

52 Dazy, *La partie et le tout*, 57. TN: Florimond Bonte speaking to the National Assembly, November 23, 1947, with a speech he had previously given in Algiers in 1943.

53 TN: The "Native Code," also referred to as *l'indigénat*, was a regime of administrative sanctions applied to colonial subjects first instituted in 1881.

54 Brochure for the Brazzaville Conference, published in Algiers, 1944, quoted in Grégoire Madjarian, *La question coloniale et la politique du parti communiste* (Paris: Maspero, 1977), 49. TN: Preamble of the draft document of the Conference, *Brazzaville: 30 janvier—8 février 1944* (Ministère des Colonies, 1944), 32. Quoted

NATIONAL INTEREST

In the final years of the Second World War, the notion of *national interest* took center stage. One might argue that liberating the country from the Nazi yoke benefited several social classes and groups: the proletariat, the peasantry, the urban petty bourgeoisie, and so on. But the concept of national interest included that of the capitalist class, whose interests were met precisely through collaborating with the Nazis; de Gaulle tried to defend this class against itself in order to somehow save it. The PCF, on the other hand, contended that the working class was *the only* class capable of representing the interests of the nation. This thesis never disappeared from the ideology of the Party leaders. In their eyes, capitalists betrayed the nation when they submitted to the Nazi boot and American imperialism, or when trusts traded on world markets. The PCF thus inverted Marx and Engels's formula in the Manifesto according to which *working men have no country.*[55] For them, capital is stateless, while workers must defend the nation, which big business has betrayed. Capital, of course, has no use for "a country," but it does have a national base; it controls a *national* State that protects its interests against the proletariat and against international competition to divide up the world. In fact, this is why the proletariat must first and foremost conquer the political power of "its own" country. And should the proletariat come to somehow embody the nation, it is because it has succeeded in rising to the *national* ruling class through the conquest of power.

The patriotic bourgeois conception of *national interest* led the PCF to claim that any weakening of French imperialism by nationalist movements in the colonies played into the hands of opposing

---

in Tony Smith, "A Comparative Study of French and British Decolonization," *Comparative Studies in Society and History* 20, no. 1 (January 1978): 73.

55   TN: Karl Marx and Frederick Engels, "Manifesto of the Communist Party (1848)," trans. Samuel Moore with Frederick Engels, in *Marx & Engels: Selected Works*, vol. 1 (Moscow: Progress Publishers, 1969), last accessed June 11, 2024, www.marxists.org/archive/marx/works/1848/communist-manifesto/cho1.htm#007.

imperialisms, and thus also weakened the proletariat in metropolitan France. The rhetoric is implacable.

THE FRENCH UNION

By supporting de Gaulle—whom Sadri Khiari describes as the strategist of the colonial counter-revolution—in his strategy to restore the "French grandeur" of the years of the resistance, the PCF affirmed the unity and indivisibility of the French Republic, *including the overseas territories*. It placed itself at the service of the *French renaissance* and of its capitalist regime. In a pamphlet entitled "Au service de la renaissance française" ["In the service of the French renaissance"], published clandestinely at the end of the war, we find this concentrate of white supremacism:

> For France, being a great power and simply continuing to exist is one and the same thing.[56]

The restoration of French grandeur meant safeguarding the colonial empire, threatened, on the one hand, by Anglo-American appetites, and, on the other, by national liberation movements labeled as "indigenous separatism." Indeed, the PCF tended to confuse these two fronts, portraying these movements as stooges of the "enemies of France." Thorez's closing address at the Xth National Congress of the PCF in June 1945 was titled "Au service de la France" ["In the service of France"]. It was an impassioned plea for the working class to "rebuild France," restore its "grandeur," and reestablish "its industrial and agricultural power" as quickly as possible, in so doing ensuring "the union of all good French people."[57] In its defense of the Union, the PCF's publications take on accents that attest to the depth of their racism and conviction that France is a superior nation

---

56 Madjarian, *La question coloniale*, 54.
57 Maurice Thorez, *Une politique de grandeur française* (Paris: Éditions Sociales, 1945), 265ff.

whose task is to civilize backward countries, "our" colonies. On this subject, Grégoire Madjarian writes:

> It was as a colonizing agent working toward reform and self-assurance of its intrinsic superiority and generosity that the PCF put forward proposals aimed at ensuring the progress of the peoples for whom France was "responsible." Lyautey's and Albert Sarrault's ideas resonated in the careful assertion that: "Despite the fruitful work of many Frenchmen in our colonies, and in particular the admirable dedication of doctors and teachers who are too few in number and inadequately equipped, the commercial exploitation of colonial territories means that our country has not sufficiently fulfilled its 'civilizing mission.'"[58]

Remarks reflecting the paternalistic conception of the relationship between the metropole and the colony are legion and circular: the metropole keeps the colony in a state of backwardness, which means it is not yet mature enough to gain independence and break away from the oppression that keeps it under tutelage. In the April 1945 issue of *Cahiers du communisme*, Henri Lozeray wrote: "The colonies ... are absolutely incapable of existing economically and, consequently, as independent nations."

In his speech to the National Assembly on September 24, 1946, Jacques Duclos drew on the Proudhonian motif of the "good" and "bad" sides to "put things in perspective":

> Just as it would be wrong, just as it would be unfair, not to make a distinction between the civilizing works accomplished in the overseas territories and the less civilizing works, it would also be unfair to deny that there have been colonial excesses .... I say this because it is a matter of tact with regard to the populations in the overseas territories. One must speak to these people in a language they can understand.[59]

---

58 Madjarian, *La question coloniale*, 160–1. Quoting Raymond Barbé, "La politique du parti et les thèses colonialistes," *Cahiers du communisme*, no. 7 (July 1946): 572.

59 Dazy, *La partie et le tout*, 43.

What tact, indeed!

The PCF continued to support the French Union even after its exclusion from government, advising colonized peoples *not to go too far down the road of freedom*[60]—that is, all the way to secession. Only when the empire began to crumble under the battering of colonized peoples did the PCF cease to use the term "French Union," formally parting with it at the XIVth Congress in July 1956. But the past would not be called into question:

> We have no doctrinal reason to abandon this term … . We have stated that our party was in favor of a true French Union, in other words, a Union freely consented to on the basis of equality and respect for the mutual interests of the peoples participating; the expression we used was intended to indicate that our party, unlike others, guaranteed, in this question as in all matters, the genuine national interest of France.[61]

MAY 8, 1945, WHEN FRANCE'S FUTURE IN THE WEST WAS AT STAKE

The PCF's defense of the French Union was more than just rhetorical. It translated into active support for the worst colonial massacres. The PCF's dramatic attitude during the Constantine massacres[62] of May 1945 owes nothing to chance, but it is sufficiently well known to be recalled only briefly here.

In 1945, the PCA and the PCF supported the repression of the Constantine movement, with the firmly held belief that "France is and must remain a great African power."[63] The year 1945 also saw

---

60   Madjarian, *La question coloniale*, 159. Citing Johanny Berlioz, "L'Afrique du Nord, foyer d'activité pro-hitlérienne et antifrançaise," *Cahiers du communisme*, no. 4 (February 1945): 47–53.

61   Georges Cogniot, report on the 14th Congress, July 18–21, 1956. Quoted in Madjarian, *La question coloniale*, 165.

62   TN: Massacres at Sétif and Guelda in Algeria, perpetrated by French colonial authorities and *pied-noir* European settler militias on May 8, 1945.

63   Florimond Bonte, speech to the Constituent Assembly, November 21, 1944. Quoted in Madjarian, *La question coloniale*, 98.

a confrontation between colonial France and the Vietnamese, who proclaimed their independence. The Việt Minh ran into a colonial wall as the Central Committee supported the Gaullist policy of reestablishing France in Indochina. The PCF clearly supported this strategy: "Indochina is one of the regions of the world where French influence cannot be contested," wrote *L'Humanité* on August 30, 1944.[64] When criticism arose following massacres performed by the expeditionary corps, it was only to advocate for less brutal methods in order to preserve the French presence. *L'Humanité* of October 13, 1945, is eloquent in this respect:

> The recent loss of French positions in Syria [which, along with Lebanon, had just proclaimed its independence] as a result of the anti-democratic policy pursued in that country, should encourage the French government not to repeat the same mistakes with regard to Indochina .... We must urgently reconsider our attitude in the Far East if we do not want the same mistakes to lead to the same harmful results.[65]

Colonial policy was not called into question, only the violent forms the reconquest of Indochina had taken. Yet the Vietnamese demanded their independence. The Vietnamese Communist government and leadership went underground and waged a war of liberation until the victory of Diên Biên Phu.

A few months later, the communist François Billoux became Minister of Defense.[66] Neither the pursuit of the colonial war in Indochina nor the repression of the Casablanca uprisings of April 7 and 8, 1947, which left over sixty dead, prompted the slightest impulse in him to resign. So many massacres were perpetrated

---

64 Madjarian, *La question coloniale*, 124.
65 Ibid., 145.
66 This position was merely symbolic, designed to test the Party's chauvinist obedience. The troops at war were commanded by the President of the Council; the real executive power was held by three other ministries: the Ministries of War, Air, and the Navy. Biloux was left only with the petrol, gunpowder, and film departments. See Madjarian, *La question coloniale*, 197–8.

with the indifference of the French people: in Thiaroye, Senegal, on December 1, 1944; in Douala, Cameroon, in September 1945, where colonists shot striking railway workers and demonstrators; in Madagascar, where the massacres began while the Communists were still in government, and where the PCF reprised the "foreign conspiracy" theory against the independence fighters:

> It is getting clearer by the day that certain foreign elements in Madagascar have not remained inactive in the events of recent weeks, and that it would not take long to find, among the auxiliaries to this plot, individuals directly linked to the Intelligence Service, agents of His Majesty the King of England, or Field Marshal Smuts.[67]

While the Malagasy people were burying their dead, Duclos expressed the Party's "deep convictions": "All of France, and I would add, all associated peoples, have an interest in France being able to maintain its positions [in the world]."[68]

The Party leaders even touted themselves as better defenders of the military than the bourgeoisie itself, demanding, in accordance with their colonial policies, that the French army be modernized. Before the National Assembly, Duclos complained that France's inadequate production of heavy armaments made the country "a second-rate power."[69] Verbal opposition to the war did not extend to refusing the means of war. On March 27, 1947, five days after the vote on military appropriation, Thorez, as vice-president of the Council, and [Paul] Ramadier signed "Instructions" for the new High Commissioner of Indochina, Émile Bollaert: if there was to be independence, it could only be conceivable within the framework of the French Union.

---

67 Raymond Barbé, "Où va l'Union française?" *Cahiers du communisme*, no. 5 (May 1947): 406–7. Quoted in Dazy, *La partie et le tout*, 44.
68 Jacques Duclos, *Journal officiel*, parliamentary debates, session of May 9, 1947. Quoted in Madjarian, *La question coloniale*, 233.
69 Ibid., March 18, 1947. Quoted in Mardjarian, *La question coloniale*, 203.

"France has interests in Indochina on the defense front which it cannot compromise on or discuss."[70] This says it all.

The PCF's positions on the Algerian War followed the same logic. They are sufficiently well known not to be expounded on here: condemnation of the November 1st uprising; difficulty in uttering the very word "independence," to which were preferred the hollower watchwords of "Peace in Algeria" or "negotiation"; refusal to help Algerian patriots on French soil. Party members were forbidden from participating in FLN support networks and providing even the slightest practical assistance. The CGT refused to make its meeting rooms available to the Union générale des travailleurs algériens and stopped printing its leaflets.[71] But proletarian internationalism cannot be reduced to vague denunciations of colonial crimes, to calls for "peace," or to providing humanitarian aid. FLN militants detained at La Santé prison made this abundantly clear to the PCF when they refused the packages they had been sent by the Secours Populaire[72] at Christmas in 1961, declaring: "If that's all the help the French working class can offer us, we'd rather do without."[73]

By acting with hostility toward insubordination and aid networks for the FLN, the Party once again cut itself off from internationalist militants. The PCF's position from the very outset of the Algerian War would drive it forever into the arms of colonial social democracy. In March 1956, the PCF voted to grant special powers to Guy Mollet, which he used to intensify murderous military operations in Algeria. The consequence proved as dramatic for the proletariat in France as for Algerian patriots: the PCF opposed the powerful movement organizing against sending out conscripts to Algeria in April 1956. As a result, strikes in factories were organized whenever a worker was "conscripted"; trains transporting soldiers were stopped; machines were halted by railway workers; train stations were ransacked; barracks (like the Reuilly barracks in Paris) were occupied; and ships were blocked through walkouts in ports. Many commu-

---

70 Madjarian, *La question coloniale*, 210.
71 Dazy, *La partie et le tout*, 64.
72 TN: Secours Populaire Français (French Popular Relief).
73 Dazy, *La partie et le tout*, 65.

nist and CGT activists took part in or initiated these struggles but were left to their own devices as PCF leadership contented itself with issuing a call for negotiations. An extraordinary opportunity to concretely oppose the colonial war was squandered. Admittedly, the initial aim was to prevent the departure of conscripted soldiers, not to obtain the withdrawal of French forces from Algeria. But such a powerful movement, with so much popular support, represented the ideal terrain for developing propaganda and policies against the colonial war.

French Communists, however, continued to justify their abdication. Thorez's arguments in *L'Humanité* on March 27, 1956, are revealing:

> The Communist Party did not wish to sacrifice the whole to the part. It subordinated its position, in a very important though limited case, to the main concern inspiring it [the Party]: preserving the possibilities for large-scale development of the united front with socialist workers, including through ceasefire and a peaceful solution to the Algerian problem.[74]

The PCF leaders' Proudhonism and opportunism can be summed up in these few lines. The Algerian War was seen as a "limited case," and the colonial question as a distant foreign policy issue that should not interfere with questions of interest to "the metropole." The interests of colonial peoples, "the part," must be subordinated to those of the French people, "the whole." Thorez imposed a distinctly colonial hierarchy on the Party's strategy. Moreover, unity with the socialist workers was subject to the latter's conditions, and they should not be inconvenienced. Finally, the objective was not independence, but "a peaceful solution."

Thorez took up the "whole and part" argument, then, as a patent of Leninism, whereas Lenin used this formula to explain that, in certain cases, a people's struggle for independence can be instrumentalized by reactionary nations and thus contradict the broader

---

74 Ibid., 72.

struggle for socialism. The "whole" here is the world revolutionary movement, and the "part," presumably, a struggle for the benefit of a reactionary power that opposes the "whole." The whole, therefore, must be favored over the part.

But what was the situation in 1956? Thorez's "whole" consisted of unity with the fringe of socialist workers who openly supported Guy Mollet's chauvinist and colonial policies (as illustrated in Algeria or during the Suez expedition with Israel), while the "part" was the Algerian revolution, which, historically, was the revolution that developed most autonomously, refusing any "tactical" or material subjection to any foreign power.

The Algerian national movement of the 1930s to 1960s rose up against one of the main imperialist powers, France, and could in no way be considered a "part" of a "whole," which would be …? The colonial status quo? Today, we hear the echoes of this position in those who would lecture us pedantically, as they defend *Françafrique*, that France is better than China. Lenin, however, advocated for "*indifference*": a member of an oppressive nation must remain "indifferent" to the question of whether a given colony belongs to "its" State or to the neighboring State.[75] What's more, and this is no small matter, Thorez justified his compromise by the need to unite with the "socialist workers." And yet, as we have seen, in the age of imperialism, the proletariat was split between a nationalist pole and a revolutionary pole: uniting with his own colonial bourgeoisie to ally with the racist part of the proletariat was certainly very coherent on Thorez's part, but it was class collaboration, and it had nothing to do with the Leninist tactic of the "part" and the "whole."

In 1945, the PCF, either in submission to Moscow's directives or out of a commitment to the social democratic solution,[76] abandoned the Communist dream. The transformation of the national

---

75 Vladimir Lenin, "The Discussion on Self-Determination Summed up" (July 1916), last accessed June 11, 2024, www.marxists.org/archive/lenin/works/1916/jul/x01.htm.

76 This is subject to debate, as Thorez's interview in *The Times* published on November 17, 1946, on "the national way" to socialism (read: the peaceful, parliamentary way, allied to social democracy) did not seem to conform to "directives

revolution into a social revolution never took place. It was then that the social/racial/colonial pact was renegotiated, with the aim of renewing and redefining the capital/labor relation between the proletariat and the bourgeoisie as an alternative to the "dictatorship of the proletariat." Social security was introduced. Workers returned to the factories. Everything was in place for France to regain its status as a Western power.

Against the backdrop of this abandonment of revolutionary ideals, the people of the left felt orphaned by the revolution. Fortunately, the "Zionist revolution" was underway, and French Communists would support and live vicariously through it, as a consolation. Whether it was to follow in the footsteps of the USSR, out of socialist enthusiasm, or out of hatred for the English—who challenged the French's sphere of influence in the East—the PCF became a "junior partner" of white supremacy ...

The rest is just the story of a shipwreck. But there are still some communists today who claim that the Party has not fallen from grace.

II. The CGT between Internationalism and Subordination to the Racial State

THE INTERNATIONALIST PHASE

Hypothesis: Workers' trade unionism is the site in which internationalism has been able to express itself and take concrete form to a far greater extent than in left-wing political organizations.

The reason for this lies in the history of the constitution of French trade unionism. With the establishment of the CGT in 1895, syndicalism took on the form of *confederated* trade unionism, that is, cross-industry, non-corporatist trade unions. It was founded to build unity across the entire class and overcome the competition between workers promoted by employers and the State as a weapon

---

from Moscow." In fact, he was harshly criticized (as well as the Italian Party) at the conference for the creation of the Cominform in September 1947.

to increase exploitation. From then on, the militant trade unionist was made to believe that any form of discrimination against one group of employees would sooner or later be harmful to the class as a whole. These notions of equality, unity, and the greater interest of the class as a whole strongly defined early confederated trade unionism, as represented by the CGT.

These values were reinforced with the adoption of the "Charter of Amiens" at the CGT's Amiens Congress in October 1906, which laid the foundations of revolutionary trade unionism. The Charter required the union to perform a dual task: on the one hand, to defend workers' immediate, day-to-day demands; on the other, to fight for the transformation of society as a whole (independently of all political parties, whatever their agendas). Article 2 of the Charter states: "Outside of all political schools, the CGT groups together all workers conscious of the fight to be carried out for the disappearance of the salaried and of employers."[77]

On this basis, internationalism could flourish.

To say that internationalism was *possible* does not mean that it has been a homogeneous and linear feature of the history of the workers' movement. Far from it, precisely because it has never, as it were, had any political outlet, but also because this internationalism stubbornly disapproved of the formation of autonomous indigenous unions, which were accused of dividing the class in the name of race.

From then on, the chauvinism that deeply characterizes the French left could only exert its deleterious influence among trade unions. Internationalism has always been the object of bitter struggle in this context, and has largely been suppressed, especially from the 1950s to the 1970s.

The most significant obstacle to the deployment of internationalism was, of course, the constitution of imperialist nation-states at the turn of the twentieth century, which established and solidified the opposition between nationals and foreigners. Since then, successive

---

77   TN: "The Charter of Amiens," voted on at the Ninth Congress of the CGT, Amiens, 1906, trans. Mitch Abidor, last accessed June 11, 2024, www.marxists.org/history/france/cgt/charter-amiens.htm.

pieces of legislation have constantly made the use of foreign labor conditional on the definition and defense of national labor interests. National preference became the organizing principle of immigration policy. This century-old State policy to control immigration was designed to identify undesirables and protect the employment of nationals. It has never been really challenged by political organizations. The attitude of CGT trade unionists toward immigrants was, from that point on, subject to dual pressures: the State's xenophobic policies and the PCF's chauvinism. The period from the 1920s to the 1930s, when internationalism found outlets within the PCF, was also marked by the actions it spurred within the union. In France, CGT trade unionism split between 1921 and 1936: the CGT's revolutionary movement (anarcho-syndicalists and communists), was forced to leave the confederation and formed the CGTU (Confédération Générale du Travail Unitaire)[78] in December 1921.

At the CGTU, internationalism could thrive. The union organized many immigrants (especially Indochinese and North African), and in September 1924, set up the First Congress of North African Workers in the Paris area. This was the era of the magazines *Le Paria* and *L'Étoile nord-africaine*,[79] which emerged in a climate conducive to internationalism. The CGTU spoke out "against all repression and limitation of immigrant labor, and for completely open borders," against deportations, and for equal pay. But—and there is a significant BUT to this incomplete internationalism—it was firmly opposed to any autonomy for non-white struggles. Black unions, for example, were quickly rebuffed when they formed independently. In a 1930 issue of *Le Réveil colonial*,[80] the CGTU strongly denounced the formation of these unions.

To the united front of the capitalists, we must necessarily oppose the united front of the workers. Unfortunately, many comrades

---

78　TN: Confédération Générale du Travail Unitaire (United General Confederation of Labor).

79　*Le Paria* and *L'Étoile Nord-africaine* are two anti-colonial newspapers published, respectively, from 1922 to 1936, and 1926 to 1937.

80　A newspaper published in Arabic by the PCF.

have not yet grasped this basic reality. And so, for some time now, we have been witnessing attempts to organize black port workers on the basis of autonomy. In Marseilles and Bordeaux, black seafarers' unions have been formed or are in the process of being formed. This movement is taking place outside of the CGTU, under the pretext of political neutrality. The CGTU and its colonial bureau cannot remain indifferent to this movement, and they denounce it as counter-revolutionary.[81]

For its part, the reformist CGT, in association with the Socialist Party (SFIO), intended to "protect the employment of nationals," following the law of 1932.[82] Trade unionism in the 1920s and 1930s clashed over the fundamental issue of the competition employers promote between workers: on the one hand, nationalist reformists felt that foreign workers should be expelled, or their numbers reduced, because they drove wages down;[83] on the other, internationalists advocated for class unity, following in the tradition of turn-of-the-century revolutionary syndicalism, and amplified by the anti-militarist and anti-imperialist struggles led by certain communists during this period.

At the CGTU's Third Confederal Congress in 1925, delegate [Julien] Racamond declared: "There is no homeland for workers, there are no foreign workers in France. There are only workers of the same country: the Proletariat!"[84]

---

81 Quoted in Philippe Dewitte, *Les mouvements nègres en France, 1919–1939* (Paris: L'Harmattan, 1985), 203. We must acknowledge, however, that the question of autonomy is never simple, and that it cannot be reduced to an abstract principle.
82 In the midst of the Great Depression, the French National Assembly passed a law on August 10, 1932, to protect the national workforce, setting a quota of 10 percent foreign workers in private companies.
83 The argument that they were scabs and hostile to strikes was often leveraged as well. This is not insignificant when we consider that the reformist CGT had opposed the major strikes organized in the wake of 1918, which was, in fact, one of the reasons for the split and the creation of the CGTU.
84 Nadir Boumaza, Ghislaine Clément, and René Gallissot, *Ces migrants qui font le prolétariat* (Paris: Méridiens-Klincksieck, 1994), 43. TN: "Rapport sur la main-d'oeuvre étrangère," presented at the congress in Paris, August 26–31, 1925, *La Vie Syndicale* (the CGTU's monthly paper), no. 18 (June 1925).

The Front Populaire would unfortunately interrupt this internationalist momentum.

THE RACIAL/NATIONAL TURN

In March 1936, the two confederations, the CGT and CGTU, reunited at the Toulouse Congress. This reunification was bound up with the alliance between the PCF and the SFIO, which resulted in May 1936 in the Front Populaire.

It should be noted that, as early as 1935, when the CGT-CGTU reunification was well underway, the last CGTU Congress (in September 1935) adopted a resolution on immigrant labor that broke with the internationalist principles of previous years: it proposed a "statute for immigrant workers" (with the stated goal of guaranteeing equal rights, but which, in reality, relegated them to a separate category within the working class), and set up a joint committee for foreign workers within (national and regional) employment offices, opening the door to control of foreign employment jointly managed with the government. On the eve of this reunification, the CGTU inched closer to the CGT's stance.

What mattered then was an antiracist (today we would call it moral antiracism) and anti-fascist "posturing," to the detriment of internationalist demands for real equality in the workplace.

The Front Populaire marked a turning point for the nationalist position (perfectly embodied, as we have seen, by Thorez), which would come to definitively dominate the Communist Party and the CGT. In 1937, Simone Weil wrote about this with concern:

We—and by *we* I mean all those, without exception, who belong to the Popular Alliance [Front Populaire)]—*we* have the same mentality as the bourgeoisie. An employer is capable of condemning his workers to the most atrocious misery and of being moved by a beggar they pass in the street. We who unite in the name of the struggle against misery and oppression, we are indifferent to the inhuman fate suffered far away by millions of men who depend on the politics of our country.[85]

FROM 1945 TO 1954: TOWARD THE ALGERIAN WAR

After Liberation, immigration changed in content, with immigrants from the colonies becoming increasingly numerous (200,000 Algerians in France in 1954 swelled to 800,000 by the end of the 1960s). Immigration became a key factor in the formation of the working class, as in the formation of trade unions and political organizations.

While the Communist movement was steeped in chauvinism, the trade union movement was able to develop internationalist positions here and there, welcoming and organizing immigrant workers, and advancing specific demands with them. Internationalist Communists also expressed their views within the trade union movement. All this was made possible by the strong commitment to the struggle of the immigrants themselves. But let's be a bit more specific.

On the one hand, the dominant line was nationalism. The CGT Congress of April 1946 outlined the program as it related to immigration (which remained unchanged in the following years, until at least 1961): the aim was, indeed, to obtain guarantees "in order to avoid competition with French workers." The union returned to the idea of developing "a democratic legal status for immigrants," and facilitating assimilation through automatic naturalization. The CGT suggested controlling the entry of foreign workers and sorting them "according to unemployment."[86]

But, on the other hand, internationalism did find outlets. It was expressed through struggle, as many Algerians were members of

---

85 Quoted in Patrice Alric, "Simone Weil 'contre le colonialisme,'" *Survie* (July–August, 2018), last accessed June 11, 2024, https://survie.org/billets-d-afrique/2018/279-juillet-aout-2018/article/simone-weil-contre-le-colonialisme. TN: Simone Weil, "Le sang coule en Tunisie," *Feuilles Libres de la Quinzaine* 3, no. 33 (March 25, 1937). Partial translation in "Blood Is Flowing in Tunisia," in *Simone Weil on Colonialism: An Ethic of the Other*, ed. and trans. J. P. Little (Lanham, MD: Rowman & Littlefield, 2003), 44. The version of the essay published in this volume differs slightly from the version cited by the author.

86 Boumaza, Clément, and Gallissot, *Ces migrants qui font le prolétariat*, 58.

the CGT and at the frontline of strikes. And politically, as well, as the CGT was clearly in favor of Algerian independence (it was the only trade union organization to hold this position[87]). The MTLD Messalistes[88] were part of the CGT in France as well as in Algeria. Immigrant workers formed, at times, the largest body of the CGT, as was the case at Renault in the 1950s. Fervor for the Algerian people's struggle for independence was vigorously expressed after the repression of the July 14, 1953 demonstration where, as in previous years, thousands of Algerian workers marched in the CGT procession with the national flag at the helm. On that day, six Algerians and one French militant—a communist member of the CGT and organizer of the demonstration—were murdered by the police.[89] In the days that followed, the seven bodies were exhibited at the Maison des Métallos—the Algerians wrapped in their national flag—and hundreds of thousands of Parisians came to pay their respects.

Another example of internationalism can be found in an Algerian militant's report on the annual congress of the FTM-CGT (metalworkers) in late November 1954:

In keeping with the CGT's tradition of proletarian internationalism, the comrades disapproved of the attitude of the government, which persists in ignoring the national aspirations of the peoples of North Africa .... They expressed the Federation's complete and total solidarity with the struggle of the peoples of North Africa for their independence. A motion to this effect was adopted by all

87 "In November 1950, the union confederation affirmed, in *Le Peuple*, its 'active solidarity with the struggle led by the valiant Algerian, Tunisian, and Moroccan people for their independence,' which "forms part of the struggle of all peoples for peace, self-determination, and better living conditions." Quoted in Laure Pitti, "La CGT et les Algériens en France métropolitaine durant les années 1950: une décennie de tournants," in *La CGT dans les années 1950*, ed. Élyane Bressol, Michel Dreyfus, Joël Hedde, and Michel Pigenet (Rennes: Presses universitaires de Rennes, 2005), 461.

88 TN: MTLD, or Mouvement pour le triomphe des libertés démocratiques (Movement for the Triumph of Democratice Liberties), led by Messali Hadj. Messalistes were supporters of the Algerian nationalist politician, Messali.

89 Abdelkader Draris, Mouhoub Illoul, Maurice Lurot, Amar Tadjadit, Larbi Daoui, Tahar Madgène, and Abdallah Bacha.

delegates. This congress was very moving; for me, as an Algerian, it embodied another face of France—the France we love, the workers' France, which we will never mistake for the France of our oppressors.[90]

Late November 1954: an important date, as the outbreak of the Algerian uprising led to serious divisions within the CGT. We know that the PCF condemned the insurrection. Some CGT sections followed this position, while others (like the metallurgy sector) supported the insurrection.

FROM 1954 TO 1968: THE ALGERIAN WAR AND THE RISE OF ANTI-IMPERIALISM AMONG WESTERN YOUTH

The struggle for Algerian independence marked a turning point. After the outbreak of the insurrection, the PCF and the PCA broke with the nationalists. This led Algerians to leave the CGT in Algeria and form the Union générale des travailleurs algériens (UGTA)[91] in agreement with the FLN in late 1955, while in France they formed the (Messalist) Union syndicale des travailleurs algériens (USTA).[92]

In France, where they were strongest, internationalist militants held firm despite their isolation. In 1958, a report from the Prefecture counted 1,500 pro-FLN militants at Renault.[93] Two positions clashed: struggle for independence and protest against the "cost of war." This marked the start of a period of trial and error for the union, which doubled down on the order to control and restrict immigration: immigrants were getting in the way. Once again, the Algerian struggle would change the course of things. After the victory of the Algerian people in 1962, the CGT's National Conference on Immigration in 1963 not only denounced racism once again, but also and especially recognized that the order to close the borders had been a mistake.

---

90 Laure Pitti, "Une matrice algérienne?" *Politix* 4, no. 76 (2006): 145.
91 TN: Union des travailleurs algériens (General Union of Algerian Workers).
92 TN: Union syndicale des travailleurs algériens (Union of Algerian Workers).
93 Pitti, "Une matrice algérienne?" 154.

Henri Krasucki[94] called for "respect for national sentiments and national characteristics" among immigrants, whereas beyond the PCF, and often in opposition to it, political internationalism was expressed by student youth in their support for the Algerian FLN and later, the Vietnamese FNL. In the 1960s, this wave of anti-imperialism took hold of youth across all Western countries.

FROM 1968 TO 1996: CONVERGING STRUGGLES

1968, a pivotal year: while immigrant workers strongly mobilized during the strikes of May and June, they were largely overlooked in the negotiations between unions, employers, and the government. And yet, in 1968, many things had changed that would later come to be significant: the vigor of anti-imperialism, for one, but also the discrediting of the PCF due to its stance on the colonial question and the anti-capitalist struggle. The strong involvement of immigrant workers in the strikes of 1968 foreshadowed the struggles of specialized workers [OS] in the 1970s. It also foreshadowed the struggle of immigrant workers (alongside French international-ist militants) to have their voices heard within the union.

The incident at the Renault factory in Billancourt during the 1968 strike is revealing in this respect. To quote Laure Pitti:

Beginning on May 25, 1968, a number of foreign workers gathered to draw up a list of demands denouncing "the confine-ment of immigrant workers to specialized jobs" and demanding the introduction of a training policy, as well as "the potential for professional development." This platform represented a group of Algerian, Portuguese, and Spanish workers, all specialized workers, some unionized with the CGT or CFDT, but also some

---

94 Polish Jew, member of the MOI [FTP-MOI: Francs-Tireurs et Partisans—Main-d'œuvre Immigrée, or Irregular Troops and Partisans—Immigrant Workforce] and the PCF, and active in the resistance from the age of sixteen. Arrested in 1943, Krasucki was tortured for six weeks without capitulating, deported to Janischowitz and later, Buchenwald, where he participated in the uprising and freed the camp. He was secretary-general of the CGT from 1982 to 1992.

non-unionized. Among the platform's initiators was Mohand Ail Aissa, one of the FLN officials at Renault during the liberation struggle.[95]

The drafters of this platform sought to disseminate it to all strikers in order to make the fight against "discrimination in employment" into a general demand. But they were turned down by the strike committee, in which the CGT held a majority.[96] The Renault CGT leaders considered it to be a marginal issue, while it was a central one for the platform's drafters. The opening lines of the platform clearly express a refusal to be assigned an "immigrant status":

The immigrant workers of the Régie Renault, fighting along-side their French comrades, reaffirm once again that they are an integral part of the French working class. Not only do they stand in solidarity with their French comrades, they are also involved in the struggle being waged by French workers for the satisfaction of their general and specific rightful demands.

The text concludes: "Long live class struggle! Long live proletarian internationalism! Long live the struggle of the workers of Régie Renault."[97]

In the years after 1968, immigration struggles expanded. First of all, major strike movements mobilized specialized workers—the most exploited section of the working class, predominantly comprising immigrants—across large companies in the metal, chemical, and automotive industries, among others. Major demands were won (regarding wages, qualification standards, monthly pay, and working conditions). Undocumented people joined the movement, demanding work permits and the regularization of their social security status. Then, the struggles expanded to questions of housing (with the large Sonacotra strikes of 1975) and equal rights.

---

95   Pitti, "Une matrice algérienne?" 158.
96   The platform was published in several militant newspapers in 1968.
97   Pitti, "Une matrice algérienne?" 160.

The unions' attitude toward immigrants speaks to a more general concern: would the PCF and CGT support and organize the most exploited section of the proletariat (specialized workers), or defend the labor aristocracy? The high proportion of immigrants among specialized workers (85 percent were specialized workers in the 1970s and 1980s) also overlapped with a racial division: white working-class aristocracy/indigenous immigrants. Specialized workers made egalitarian demands (the same wage increases for all) that challenged the hierarchical structures defended by the white worker (who was in favor of hierarchical pay raises). They led difficult struggles (occupation, refusal to return to work) that had a major impact. Their demands went beyond wages to extend to issues around the organization of work, training, and recognition of length of service. The success of this powerful strike movement of the early 1970s led to a change in hierarchical classifications that benefited specialized workers, and to the affirmation of equal professional rights: it forced the unions (beyond just militant internationalists) to admit that immigrants "are from here," that they work here, and that they intend to stay whatever the employment situation, and on an equal footing with French workers. The question of competition was therefore settled by refusing to "protect French labor" and asserting equal rights.

It's safe to say that, at that point, the labor movement could no longer go back on the issue. This is due to the convergence of the May–June '68 movement and the assault on capital launched by immigrant specialized workers in the years that followed. During this period, workers took their struggle into their own hands when the unions were reluctant to follow. They often imposed the formation of strike committees, as well as their presence in negotiations.

This autonomy was also asserted during the major struggles led by the Sonacotra tenants, which lasted from 1975 to 1979. In 1978, at the height of the movement, nearly half of the tenants had stopped paying rent. They denounced excessive rent, management's general attitude, and their lack of freedoms. More fundamentally, the immigrants living there demanded to be recognized as autonomous tenants in their own right, rather than as workers "housed in accommodations" under the supervision of the employers' henchmen.

The unions kept their distance from the movement. The CFDT eventually joined in, followed by the CGT, which denounced the fierce repression suffered by the rent strikers (eviction, seizure and suspension of wages, non-renewal of residence permits, deportation).

The strike failed, but it had a profound impact on immigrants, who became aware of their power and of the need to organize their own struggle if French organizations failed to rise to the occasion.

This movement was not linear, and there were occasional regressions. In the early 1980s, the PCF continued to make the connection between immigration and unemployment. A 1985 pamphlet, *Le PCF et l'immigration*, reads: "The Communist Party is opposed to the deportation of immigrants with legal residency. But the law must apply to all. Offenders, wherever they may come from, should be deported with respect for their dignity"[98]—which is precisely the position Fabien Roussel[99] maintains today. Once again, we can see that trade unionism was more advanced than the "political process," in part because of the presence of the Maoist far left, which mobilized in support of a "multinational people" (a "people" made up of those who are from here).

Against the backdrop of the great worker mobilizations of 1968 and the 1970s, which profoundly changed conditions for wage-earners, the anti-colonial struggle was led primarily by immigrant workers, in alliance with internationalist militants (both among the youth and in the trade unions). Kristin Ross writes: "[By 1968 the sky was already darkened]. It was an event with a long preparation, dating back to the mobilization against the Algerian War and with an immediate afterlife continuing at least up to the mid-1970s."[100]

---

98 Boumaza, Clément, and Gallissot, *Ces migrants qui font le prolétariat*, 141.
99 TN: Fabien Roussel has been the national secretary of the PCF since 2018.
100 Kristin Ross, *May '68 and Its Afterlives* (Chicago: University of Chicago Press, 2022), 26.

THE TALBOT STRIKES (1982–84), OR THE BROKEN
ALLIANCE OF "THE SICKLE AND THE KORAN"

These strikes concerned specialized workers, the most precarious workers laboring under the harshest conditions—most of them Moroccan, since French employers found them to be more "docile." Some have spoken of an "immigrant May '68," which may be justified given the scale and duration of the movement. Vincent Gay has described them as strikes for dignity.[101] Demands included better working conditions in factories, where a harsh and paternalistic managerial climate reigned, as well as time for prayer and accommodations for work during Ramadan. The strike gained ground because the left was in power, but the PS was hostile to these movements, denouncing the strikers as "Shiites," Muslims "foreign to the economic realities of France." The State feared this strike because it was political; it took aim at neoliberal modernity, in a way, in part by making demands related to Muslim religious practice. The relationship between these demands and the workers' demands supported by the CGT caused the government to fear the country's destabilization. This is why the right would denounce an alliance "between the sickle and the Koran" during the 1983 municipal elections.

At the same time, other white workers' struggles were collapsing into bitter defeat: take the steel industry in Longwy, for instance, or the miners' strike in Great Britain. There was no alliance between these movements. The break between rednecks and barbarians was clear. The latter would be referred to exclusively as "Muslims," "Islamists," or "immigrants," but not as "workers," while the former were branded as Lepenists. Between 1968 and 1996, Talbot confirmed the schism among the (inter)national proletariat. Moral antiracism ratified it. This would be a moment of nepotistic accession which not even the events at Saint-Bernard could prevent.

---

101   TN: Vincent Gay, *Pour la dignité: Ouvriers immigrés et conflits sociaux dans les années 1980* (Lyon: Presses universitaires de Lyon, 2021).

1995–96: SAINT-BERNARD

In the 1980s, the so-called "second generation" took up the fight against deportations, police killings, racism, and the struggle for rights, culminating in the 1983 March for Equality and Against Racism.

The great strike movement of December 1995 had a major impact on all the wage-earners who had rallied around the strikers. New unemployment organizations took part in the general assemblies and, while the strikers came mainly from public services— which few immigrants worked in—it can be said that this is when the progressive trade union movement (CGT, SUD[102]) definitively rejected competition between workers, not just in words, but in actions. The year 1994 saw the alliance of youth and adults against the CIP,[103] and the alliance of wage-earners and the unemployed (a large demonstration for the latter took place in June 1994). At the end of the December 1995 movement, several organizations, unions, and immigrant associations met at Beaubourg and launched L'Appel des sans.[104] In March 1996, in the wake of this call, one of the largest movements of undocumented people was initiated with the occupation of the church of Saint-Ambroise. On June 28, the hundreds of "Saint-Ambroise" undocumented people (who had occupied the church on March 18) left rue Pajol to occupy the church of Saint-Bernard. On July 5, ten went on a hunger strike. On August 12, at 6 a.m., 300 CRS[105] evacuated the strikers, who were forcibly hospitalized. The same day, Louis Viannet, general secretary of the CGT, visited the undocumented people at Saint-Bernard. He was the first national figure to do so. On August 23, despite the mobilization

---

102   TN: SUD, or Solidaires-Unitaires-Démocratiques, is a French group of trade unions.
103   TN: CIP stands for Contrat d'insertion professional (Professional Insertion Contract), a fixed-term or temporary employment contract for people under the age of twenty-six, remunerated at 80 percent of minimum wage and implemented under Prime Minister Édouard Balladur's government.
104   TN: "L'Appel des sans" translates most literally to the "call of the without."
105   TN: CRS stands for Compagnies Républicaines de Sécurité (Republican Security Corps), the general reserve of the French National Police.

of hundreds of "supporters," the undocumented were violently evicted from Saint-Bernard by 1,100 CRS and mobile guards.

On September 4, at the CGT's "kick-off meeting" at Le Zénith, 5,000 people gave Madjiguène Cissé a standing ovation following her speech on behalf of the undocumented at Saint-Bernard. These events marked an important step in the position of France's leading trade union—a moment when its long-contained internationalism could be expressed in action, not without difficulty but with much determination. And it is no coincidence that class unity was first able to affirm itself within the trade union movement. As Madjiguène Cissé has noted, "This was a turning point in the history of French trade unionism, which has, at times, called for the deportation of foreign workers."[106] Perceptively, she nuanced her remarks with a critique that shed light on the intentions of the French left: "External issues having to do specifically with the organizations that supported us, with their political positions, could begin to influence the nature of our struggle."[107] Indeed, the occupation of Saint-Ambroise took place a few months after a proposal was advanced to reform social security, pitting the Juppé government against French workers even as the Front National celebrated its electoral victories. Madjiguène Cissé rightly feared that the white left's support had more to do with general objectives unrelated to the immediate goals of the undocumented workers, and that, in the long term, the direction of the struggle would escape them.

She was right, of course. This is what all non-white autonomous organizations fear from experience. It is a concern that is constantly reanimated to the point of paranoia, given that the subordination of indigenous struggles is an invariant of the white political field.[108]

---

106 Madjiguène Cissé, *Paroles de sans-papiers* (Paris: Dispute, 1999), 216.

107 Madjiguène Cissé, quoted in Khiari, *Pour une politique de la racaille*, 72.

108 TN: For Bouteldja, the white political field "designates the space, times, and political logics in imperialist states or in the global interstate system that are structured, especially in their institutional incarnations, by past and present conflicts within the official white group as well as by modes of monopolizing the political arena developed by this same official white group." See Houria Bouteldja, "Party of the Indigenous of the Republic (PIR) Key Concepts," trans. Paola Bacchetta, *Critical Ethnic Studies* 1, no. 1 (Spring 2015): 27.

But we have also seen that the realm of trade unions, caught between the racial State and nationalist communism, and plagued by its own chauvinistic ambivalences, was transformed under the blows of indigenous power. If this indigenous power could better flourish within trade unions, it is also because there was greater recognition of their rights as a workforce and, it bears repeating, because there was greater awareness of the common interests they shared with their white counterparts. Though not to the point of dissolving the racial consciousness of the latter, which the social pact continued to nurture relentlessly. Far from it.

French "political society" cannot, of course, be reduced to these two major organizations that constitute its main leftist historical expression. Yet, it must be stated that "political society" would not be so strongly bound to the racial State if "civil society"—that is, "the people" in all its various states and components, but above all understood through its constitutive unit, the individual citizen—was not itself determined, in its most intimate affects, by a strong white consciousness. It is a people composed of white citizen-individuals *objectively* produced by the history of the imperialist racial State, but also a *subjectively* consenting people, without whom the racial State could not be characterized as "integral." Let's proceed.

Race and Civil Society

I'm Nobody! Who are you?
Are you—Nobody—too?
Then there's a pair of us!
Don't tell! they'd advertise—you know!

How dreary—to be—Somebody!
How public—like a Frog—
To tell one's name—the livelong June—
To an admiring Bog![1]

— Emily Dickinson, "I'm Nobody! Who are you?"

To vote in a Western democracy is to cast a blank vote.

When one fulfills one's "electoral duty" in France, Great Britain, or the United States, one casts a blank vote, because choice is exercised within the ideological boundaries established by the white political field, which is, by definition, enclosed on all sides by class division and, so to speak, horizonless. And yet, the characterization of class division as white[2] indicates that it bears a color and that the battle between the bourgeoisie and the people, as ferocious as it may be, respects the racial/colonial paradigm that closes in on the political field like a corset. Disunited by antagonistic class relations, the two battling blocs are united by race. A civil society that is birthed from this history is therefore branded by the colors of white compromise, which it must be subjected to for lack of daring

---

1   Emily Dickinson, "I'm Nobody! Who are you? (1861)" (260), in *The Poems of Emily Dickinson*, ed. Ralph W. Franklin (Cambridge, MA: The Belknap Press of Harvard University, 1999), 116.

2   See Sadri Khiari, *Pour une politique de la racaille: Immigré-e-s, indigènes et jeunes de banlieues* (Paris: Textuel, 2006).

and imagination, and which it must validate out of an instinct for self-preservation.

Judge for yourselves.

A vote for the far right is a vote for white supremacy, the watchdog of the bourgeoisie.

A vote for the right is a vote for the imperialist bourgeoisie.

A vote for the institutional left is a vote for bourgeois reformism.

A vote for the Communist Party is a vote for class collaboration.

A vote for the far left is rare.

To vote is to cast a blank vote …

It is no secret, except for the naive, that democracy has been placed at the service of the bourgeois State. We all know that the electoral system is designed to temper revolutionary ardor and compel popular consensus. It is sufficiently well established that universal suffrage is the ultimate form of legitimation of order, and voting the political act par excellence at the service of the hegemony of the ruling class; I need not spill more ink over this. On the other hand, the fact that this system—which results from a constant, violent power struggle between the racial/bourgeois State and political society—can generate a democratic system, and thus a civil society strongly defined by white desires, is less obvious when considered only through the lens of class. This lens is critical but incomplete if we take into consideration the blind spots of the electoral gesture and its racial determinants.

While the first article of the Declaration of the Rights of Man stipulates that "men are born free and remain equal in rights," the racial State, dominated by capitalist logic, has no intent to apply these principles or emancipate anyone. Quite the contrary, in fact. It favors compromise over arbitrariness and authoritarianism (to which it resorts when necessary). Universal suffrage is one such compromise. On the one hand, the right to vote is gradually extended to the working classes and then to women (who had to fight hard to obtain it); on the other, safeguards are put in place to restrict available choices to what is within the bounds of national interest. The "free" and "equal" individual is free to make a choice that emanates only from the white political field, and to believe in formal equality—the kind that exonerates bourgeois Whites from social justice and real equality with petty Whites,[3] and exonerates petty Whites from real equality with non-Whites. The value of abstractions …

> Man must be as independent as possible from other men and as dependent as possible on the State.[4]

Now, this could shed new light on the "Liberty, Equality, Fraternity" triptych birthed by the French Revolution.

Liberty.

Man's dependence on the State seemed to signal a step forward at the time of the Revolution. In retrospect, we have reason to doubt it. Freedom means separation and captivity. First, you separate yourself from your fellow men; you dismantle your camp, weaken your power, and surrender yourself to the State as an individual, a citizen, an atom … as less than nothing. But not without pride. For the individual-citizen, born of the bowels of modernity, thinks and is. They can be recognized by the form and lightness of this phrasing, which is quick to escape from the mouth of any smug person—"Personally, I think that …"—whenever they are given the opportunity to mumble a thought about the State, repeat a commonplace, or pontificate on the most hackneyed clichés. We can laugh about it with Spinoza, who ironizes from beyond the grave:

> Further conceive, I beg, that a stone, while continuing in motion, should be capable of thinking and knowing, that it is endeavouring, as far as it can, to continue to move. Such a stone, being

---

3 TN: The term *petits Blancs*, which translates literally to "little Whites," refers, in the context of the Haitian Revolution, to the poor, white merchant/worker lower/underclass of Saint-Domingue—some slave-owning, but far less well-off than the wealthy planters. This translation takes some liberties with the term, opting for "petty Whites" to echo the usage of the word "petty" in "petty bourgeoisie," which may resonate with some familiarity to an anglophone readership, but also to try to carry Bouteldja's tone into English.

4 Jean-Jacques Rousseau, quoted in Nicos Poulantzas, *State, Power, Socialism* (London: Verso, 2014 [1978]), 82.

conscious merely of its own endeavour and not at all indifferent, would believe itself to be completely free, and would think that it continued in motion solely because of its own wish. This is that human freedom, which boasts that they possess, and which consists solely in the fact that men are conscious of their own desire, but are ignorant of the causes whereby that desire has been determined.[5]

There is, then, an enigma still to be solved. Why did the French Revolution, which marked the end of feudalism and freed the people from the vassalage to which they seemed condemned for all eternity, give rise to a civil society made up of individuals separated from one another? Why did they agree to entrust their sovereignty to a State that would act as guarantor and even as custodian of their rights and liberties, thus engendering another form of vassalage? Didn't Robespierre proclaim the very first right as the right to existence? "What is freedom without the right to existence?" he repeated in chorus with all the sans-culottes. Anything that ensures the preservation of existence is the common property of society as a whole. As we all know, the liberty of human rights began with the liberty of private property. Private property lies at the heart of the bourgeois project, and it's here that History took a wrong turn. Article 2 of the Constitution of 1789 states that "the aim of all political association is the preservation of the natural and imprescriptible rights of man. These rights are liberty, property, safety, and resistance to oppression."[6] And in the Constitution of 1795: "Property is the right to enjoy and to dispose of one's goods, income, and the fruit of one's labor and industry."

Having been confiscated by the owning class, the notion of individual freedom found itself, at the foundation of civil society, reduced

5   Spinoza, Letter to G. H. Schaller (The Hague, October 1674), *Selected Correspondence of Benedict de Spinoza*, letter 62, last accessed June 11, 2024, www.faculty.umb.edu/gary_zabel/Courses/Spinoza/Texts/Spinoza/let6258.htm.
6   TN: "Declaration of the Rights of Man," approved by the National Assembly of France, August 26, 1789. See the Yale Law School Avalon Project, last accessed June 11, 2024, https://avalon.law.yale.edu/18th_century/rightsof.asp.

to a multitude wherein each entity is separated from the other and connected to the State by an invisible thread. If we persist in searching for the idealistic dimension of liberty such as it has taken shape in the integral State, we may find it either in an apolitical form, in the mouth of any demagogue, or in a revolutionary form, but only among those who conceive it as a project turned toward the future, rather than as a past or present reality.

Equality.

Is the abolition of class, race, and gender relations a condition for concrete equality? It would seem not. It is the egalitarian right to the liberty to own, to self-interest, to individualism. All these "liberties" are guaranteed and protected by the State and its police. The State protects the self-interest of each and every individual, all the while exalting it. All that remains of civil society, which has failed its political destiny, are individuals competing with one another, oblivious to their social power, to their consignment to the camp of the exploited. Equality is also, and above all, the erasure (not the abolition) of class, race, and gender divisions produced by a rhetorical illusion. Is this a reality produced by the Revolution or a projection, an ideal toward which we are striving? We know the answer to this question, but French citizens on the left, and even sometimes on the right, are rather proud of the word.

Fraternity.

A superfluous word. A supplement of soul, at best. For the citizens of a bourgeois State are never brothers and sisters. They are, at best, aspiring bourgeois. Since this privilege is granted only to a minority, they will be white by compensation. In this way, they not only distance themselves from their own camp, but also and above all from the generic humanity against which they constitute themselves as white. The wretched of the earth know it well as those who can call anyone but a white person "brother." Try calling a white person "brother" and you will see how they feel attacked. Best case scenario, they will feel a vague sense of unease, as if deep down inside they knew themselves undeserving of this title and generosity. Or else, they will fear the price to pay for the advent of this brotherhood. And that's even worse.

It could be said that the real meaning of the triptych "Liberty, Equality, Fraternity"—that is, its meaning informed by capitalist/imperialist power struggles, rather than its idealistic meaning, which is genuinely revolutionary but has been crushed by the progress of bourgeois hegemony—constitutes the ideological driving force behind the integration of civil society into the integral racial State. One gradually renounces belonging to the human species to belong instead to a race, renounces class identity to adopt a national identity, renounces the collective to embrace the individual.

The affects of the individual who forms the multitude of civil society mirror the superstructure of this State:

The white citizen will vote for empire.

The French citizen will vote for national/racial preference.

The individual citizen will vote for their own interests, not those of their neighbors. Hence the polling booth, which guarantees the total fulfillment of their selfishness.

In addition, to return to Rousseau's formulation, as a citizen and dependent of the State, the individual will beg for their rights and means of survival, like a chick beckoning its mother, and this will make of them a beggar. Independent from their fellow citizens, the individual will shy away from solidarity and the common good. Proud to have torn themselves away from communal, religious, and political allegiances, the individual will boast of being a "free electron" and deprive themselves of the collective force they could represent. And when they finally take action, they will be like the famous hummingbird, doing their part.[7] Big deal!

---

7 TN: According to the legend ("La légende du Colibri"), during a large forest fire, as all the other animals fled in fear, only the hummingbird, rushing back and forth to a source of water to gather a few drops of water at a time, tried to extinguish it. When another animal pointed out the futility of the bird's efforts, the hummingbird replied, "I know, but I am doing my part." The legend was popularized by French farmer and environmentalist Pierre Rabhi as an allegory for the importance

In short, to recap:

A vote for the right is a vote for the imperialist bourgeoisie.

A vote for the institutional left is a vote for bourgeois reformism.

A vote for the Communist Party is a vote for class collaboration.

A vote for the far left is rare.

To vote is to cast a blank vote, even though white affects are variously aired in the political arena according to the respective subjectivities that populate the left/right, far-left/far-right divide.

To vote is to cast a blank vote ... except when—Oh, Irony—the ballot is blank. Though it may be risky to attribute a definitive and unequivocal meaning to the refusal to vote (whether through blank or invalid votes, or abstention), we can at least credit some of the abstainers with having eminently political morals, and consider their "civic poverty" as merely an act of revolt against an apparatus that organizes impotence, prevents any kind of reform, and allows capitalism and its advanced stage, imperialism, to develop without risk. An act of revolt, then, against an institutional vampire that produces apathy while celebrating the coronation of the citizen-voter. A complete mockery that won't fool the true idealists.[8]

One might, however, wonder about the marginality of the far left—the least white movement in the political arena by virtue of its internationalist commitment—as an electoral choice. Why does its political platform remain so unappealing to the most revolutionary elements at a time when the working classes are being sacrificed on the altar of triumphant liberalism, and even violently suppressed? What explains this disaffection, when the far left is probably the political movement most devoted to the interests of workers and most consistent in its critique of the capitalist system? There's no simple answer, but the following hypothesis could be advanced: the far left is too white for decolonial activists, and not white enough for the citizen of French stock, child of the integral racial State. It is too internationalist and too antiracist. It doesn't just defend the

---

of taking individual action as part of the collective efforts against environmental devastation.

8   A position I cannot claim for myself, as I advocate for a tactical approach to the electoral system.

interests of "rednecks," it also defends those of "barbarians"; it doesn't just defend the interests of nationals, it also defends immigrants and undocumented people; it doesn't just defend the French, it also defends oppressed peoples. It does not seek accommodations with capitalism, it wants its abolition. It is generous, which is not the least of its qualities, but as a result, it enters into direct collision with individualism and the spirit of property.[9] In short, it wants—at times, unwittingly—the end of the system that produces Whites. In short, it betrays its race. And the voter knows it. But this is not its only flaw. In fact, the far left is incapable of capturing the affects of petty Whites; it doesn't know how to communicate with them. It doesn't know how to say "we" the proles, "we" the petty Whites. It says "they" when it speaks of the people it claims to defend. The far left doesn't know how to be a part of it.

In its defense, we should recognize that white people's affects are laden with negativity. Their affects are the product of 500 years of Western military, economic, ethical, and philosophical domination. They are built around civilizational superiority, nationalism, and individualism. And what remains of the positivity, solidarity, and generosity of the petty Whites can be found more so in what makes them "Petty" than what makes them "White." It can be found in their most prestigious and heroic histories—the sans-culottes, the communards, the early communists, the internationalists, the recusants of the Algerian and Indochina wars, the resistance fighters, the "suitcase carriers"[10]—without whom France would not have a soul. But symbolic reaffiliation alone won't do because these figures, these nuisances, underwent a deep transformation and became patriots. In the process, they confirmed their own powerlessness. They will

---

9   TN: Voltaire writes, "The spirit of property doubles a man's strength. He labors for himself and his family both with more vigor and pleasure than he would for a master." See Voltaire, "Property," in *A Philosophical Dictionary*, vol. 9, trans. William F. Flemming, Project Gutenberg, 2011, last accessed June 11, 2024, www.gutenberg. org/files/35629/35629-h/35629-h.htm.

10   TN: French left-wing militants who helped the Algerian National Liberation Front (FLN) operating in the French metropolitan territory during the Algerian War, mainly by carrying money and papers for Algerians (the term goes back to the French resistance movement during the Second World War).

only become full-fledged nuisances once again when whiteness has been abolished, which requires a clean break with the racial collaboration between Bourgeois Whites and their Petty counterparts: for the Petties to join the camp of the Petty and the Pettiest, and for this act to be *desirable*.

This terrain is a minefield because petty Whites will then have to combat their own strabismus, which pushes them to fight against both the high and the low, the rich and the indigenous. It is a minefield because petty Whites will have to face up to their deepest trauma: the admission that what revolts them most is not the fact that there are poorer and more illegitimate people than themselves, but that the indigenous, *in spite of it all*, have figured out how to preserve a part of their beings, their identities, their histories. And the fact that the indigenous would die to preserve these attributes, which petty Whites have sacrificed to serve the empire—infantrymen[11] from the very start. It is unbearable for them to acknowledge their own immense loneliness and cultural impoverishment—which some have referred to as "cultural insecurity" and for which the indigenous are cynically blamed, when in fact it is produced by big business. Theirs is a culture the petty White has abandoned in exchange for a poisoned gift passed down by generations of the bourgeoisie: the gift of whiteness, which is neither a culture nor a tradition, aesthetic, spirituality, or form of transcendence. It is but a hole, an abyss into which the petty White will continue to fall indefinitely if they fail to confront the only question worth asking: who am I under my white coat?

---

11   TN: In French, *tirailleur*: infantryman trained to skirmish ahead of the main columns. The term came to refer to indigenous infantry recruited in the French colonial territories during the nineteenth and twentieth centuries, or for metropolitan units serving in a light infantry role.

Birthing the White Political Field

Deep down, I've made Gramsci's analysis my own.[1]
—Nicolas Sarkozy, a few days before the first round
of the 2007 presidential election

The integral racial State is not a totalitarian State. On the contrary. In France, it (still) exists under its democratic, liberal, social, Republican, and secular form. The proof: many generations of undesirables live within this integral racial State and are "tolerated." They come from colonies past or present and make up an important part of the proletariat. What's more, they reproduce and project themselves into it. While their integration takes the form of inclusion/exclusion, it is no less effective. And their standard of living, which is structurally below that of white France, is tendentially higher than that of their brothers and sisters back home. What's more, this State, whose authoritarian impulses advance as its democratic dimension weakens, nevertheless continues to attract the "misery of the world." For, contrary to what detractors of bourgeois democracy claim, the rule of law and democracy are not chimeras but tangible realities without which white consensus would be untenable.

The indigenous are an integral part of this State: First, by serving as "factory fodder," a poorly paid workforce entrusted with essential productive and reproductive tasks. Second, as collateral but very real beneficiaries of the legacy of the French Revolution, the Enlightenment, and the achievements of class struggle. And finally, as agents in their own struggles to improve, for better or for worse, the conditions of their assimilation, both outside the white political field (when they claim their autonomy) and within it (when they accept its conditions).

---

1   Reported by *Le Figaro*, April 17, 2007.

The integral racial State is not a totalitarian State, because the consensus of whiteness, including in the form of racial tolerance, ensures its continuity. Thus, even the most subaltern and despised classes find some benefit in it, provided they know how to stay in their place.

We can now better understand what Gramsci meant by "pessimism of the intellect"—Gramsci, for whom the State was "an outer ditch, behind which there stood a powerful system of fortresses and earthworks," "hegemony protected by the armour of coercion."[2] It is a convolution of consent and coercion at the service of the hegemony of the ruling classes that must be confronted—starting with the knot that is white supremacy, which unites big business, the modern State, and the white working classes.

The existence of the integral racial State is indissociable from the history of slavery, colonization, and Western imperialism. While capitalism was born of the power politics of nation-states, and while nation-states gained power (to destroy, to conquer) thanks to modern capitalism, race is, as we have seen, one of the pillars of the "geopolitical logics of power" according to which a hierarchical division between dominating nations (which rival each other) and dominated nations (which are the former's hunting ground) play out on a global scale. The stakes are high: capitalist valorization and the power politics of nation-states revolve around race.

Thus, the racial State is inseparable from the ongoing and determined struggle of the ruling classes for hegemony over the State. It is inseparable from the class struggle in which it is refracted and on which it leaves its mark, just as it is inseparable from racial struggle (against slavery, segregation, apartheid, colonialism, policing, discrimination ...). Racial interests and the struggles they provoke have, however, been crushed and occluded by the division that opposes the bourgeoisie to one of the groups it exploits, the white proletariat. We know this division as the left/right opposition. It swallows up all

---

2   TN: Antonio Gramsci, *Selections from the Prison Notebooks of Antonio Gramsci*, ed. and trans. Quintin Hoare and Geoffrey Nowell Smith (New York: International Publishers, 1971), 238, 263.

other conflicts and appears as the only way of structuring the political field; its self-evidence is virtually naturalized. Rarely investigated as the product of specific historical power relations, it appears all the more universal. In short, the history of modernity is a history of class struggle, which has been its driving force. Fair enough! This is an indisputable truth, but it would be more accurate to say that class struggle—in its concrete materializations—is the form that the conflict between white exploiters and the white exploited has taken, subsumed under a global system of racial domination. Class conflict only takes shape in relation to the coloniality of power on a global scale.

If an integral racial State exists, then the political field that organizes this specific conflictuality also exists. The first gives rise to the second. This is what we have called "the White political field."[3] To continue to approach the latter solely through the prism of a globalized, homogeneous class struggle is to maintain a confused perspective on the materiality of North/South relations of domination, and on the unity between Whites made possible by this domination. On the contrary, to identify the existence of a white political field that structures the conflict among Whites just as much as their unity—i.e., the overcoming of class conflict through white supremacism—brings to light the domination of the ruling classes over their respective States, but also over the global inter-state system. This hegemony is maintained and continually renewed because it rests on a solid structure, wherein adherence from both political and civil society outweighs distrust and opposition. In France, this consensus calls itself "Republican." But there can be no adherence without shared interests, reciprocity, and active complicity on all sides.

This is why we remain perplexed by the somewhat well-received analyses that present racism first and foremost as a "passion from above."[4] These analyses would have us forget that racism is not a

---

3 See Sadri Khiari, *Pour une politique de la racaille: Immigré.e.s, indigènes et jeunes de banlieues* (Paris: Textuel, 2006).

4 Jacques Rancière, "Racism: A Passion from Above," trans. Jonathan Collerson, *Monthly Review Online*, September 23, 2010, last accessed June 11, 2024, https://

conjunctural "passion," and even less a sentiment. It is a system. It has structured the formation of modern States since the very beginning, and it is the material translation of an effective, if asymmetrical agreement. The consensus of the white masses is obtained through their integration into the circuit of wealth redistribution, through a genuine relationship to the nation—which owes them security and national preference, and to which they owe loyalty and patriotism—and through their elevation to the rank of indebted "citizens" nonetheless endowed with "inalienable" rights. From this point of view, as Sadri Khiari points out,

> it seems completely irrational to assert that the white working classes are not racist, but rather simply idiotic receptacles for the ruling classes' sales patter, designed to distract them from class struggle. In these times of crisis, the white working classes are defending their "gains," one of which is to be white.[5]

Yet Jacques Rancière is partly right when he affirms that,

> a lot of energy has been spent against a certain figure of racism—embodied in the *Front National*—and a certain idea that this racism is the expression of "white trash" (*"petits Blancs"*) [sic] and represents the backward layers of society. A substantial part of that energy has been recuperated to build the legitimacy of a new form of racism: state racism and "Leftist" intellectual racism.[6]

Even though the quotation marks around the word "Leftist"—which attempt to underline an antinomy between leftism and racism—are

---

mronline.org/2010/09/23/racism-a-passion-from-above, based on the talk, "Les Roms, et qui d'autre?" September 11, 2010, published by *Mediapart* as "Racisme, une passion d'en haut," September 14, 2010, last accessed June 11, 2024, https://blogs.mediapart.fr/edition/roms-et-qui-dautre/article/140910/racisme-une-passion-den-haut, and in *Les trente inglorieuses* (Paris: La fabrique, 2022), 57–62.

5   TN: Sadri Khiari, "Nous avons besoin d'une stratégie décoloniale," in *Race et capitalisme*, ed. Félix Boggio Éwanjé-Épée and Stella Magliani-Belkacem (Paris: Edition Syllepse, 2012), 157.

6   Rancière, "Racism: A Passion from Above."

unnecessary, it is indeed unfair to accuse only the "white trash," whom a large part of the intellectual and political left has long stigmatized as tendentially more racist than middle-class society. But while it would be unfair to blame them for this, it would also be unfair to exonerate them. In fact, they represent one of the three agents in the equation that has led to the advent of the integral racial State. Neither their idiocy nor their intelligence comes into play here. Only the awareness of their immediate interests.

This agent, however, is the weakest link in the equation. "Rednecks," who represent a subaltern section of political society and a large section of civil society, are the least reliable category of the Republican consensus. This is where the partly true idea that racism is a "passion from above" might have deserved further inquiry. The fact that the Western ruling classes have a vital interest—and I weigh my words carefully here—in maintaining both white supremacy on a global scale, and racial tensions within nation-states, is undeniable. The fact that these tensions are continuously fueled by the parties, organizations, and intellectuals representing the owning class and the ideological apparatus of the State is self-evident. The fact that the media acts as the driving force of State racism is glaringly obvious. We can only, therefore, agree with this point of view: "In fact, it is not the government that acts under the pressure of popular racism and in reaction to the so-called 'popular' passions of the extreme-right [sic]. The State's aim [*raison d'État*] is to maintain this other to whom it entrusts the imaginary determination of what it actually legislates."[7] A casual observer of French politics can only conclude that Islamophobia is the favorite sport of the French elite. Its absolutely uninhibited nature is manifest everywhere, and racist one-upmanship is justified in the name of social realism, while insults, caricatures, and the stigmatization of non-white populations are held up as veritable editorial virtues, according to which the courage to tell the truth is matched only by innocent intentions. In times of crisis—in this case, the decline of France as a world power—the State strengthens its grip on economic and social levers

---

7   Ibid.

even as it becomes more authoritarian, restricting liberties and chipping away at democratic principles. The ideological apparatuses are running at full power in order to, on the one hand, strike down the idea that "there are no alternatives," and on the other, maintain racial tension at an all-time high to build a firewall between the white and non-white working classes. Racial conflict is all the more important in that it helps to recreate unity among Whites whenever the social pact is called into question by the unleashing of liberal policies.

And yet, it is precisely because maintaining a firewall between Whites and non-Whites requires agents of the racial/imperial order to be in a permanent state of alert that "rednecks" emerge as the weakest link in the equation. Consensus needs to be stoked; so too does the flame of racism. But ultraliberal policies shortchange the social pact and betray the white working classes, in part because of decreasing imperial annuities. The ruling classes know they can count on nationalist affects to orient the revolt against non-Whites, but these affects are not always shared equally and homogeneously among all the white subaltern classes. Some have been won over by the far right, others by the Republican parties, others still by the far left, and others abstain—disillusioned and resigned. The uprising of the Gilets Jaunes is a perfect illustration of this. Like the State, the Gilets Jaunes tend to express racist, homophobic, and sexist sentiments. But these are not the passions that dominated their uprising. Programmed to regard the indigenous as their intimate enemy, they escaped this fate and jammed the machine by attacking the State and its representatives. The "system" is to blame, they argued, as well as the decline in their purchasing power and the democratic institutions that betrayed and denigrated them. Let's wager that if Islamophobia developed at the end of the 1980s,[8] it is because of the blows from the struggles led by the "second generation," which refused assimilation and demanded equality, but also because of the looming first Gulf War, which demanded

---

8 For example, with the Creil case in 1989, when three schoolgirls were expelled for wearing headscarves.

national unity. If Islamophobia surged in the early 2000s, it was not only because of the need to reestablish white power after the September 11th attacks—which were viewed as a real warning shot against Western imperialism—but also to deal with pension reform. If the law against separatism[9] was passed in 2021, it is because it had become necessary to recreate the sacred union after both the Gilets Jaunes insurrection—which was dangerously indifferent to the indigenous—and the emergence of the "Adama Generation"[10] mobilized against the Republican police and poised to rouse white sympathies, especially among the people on the left and the Gilets Jaunes insurgents, who had themselves been severely brutalized by that same police. This is because whiteness, among Whites, and petty Whites in particular, is neither an absolute nor an ontological fact. It is a social relation constantly reproduced by the forces that privilege it, a social relation shaped by the forces that oppose it. Thus, Whites cannot be reduced to their whiteness, and whiteness materializes variously depending on their social and geographic background, political orientation, gender, and age. Throughout the long history of the formation of capital, Whites have allied with their State, but they are not entirely its captives, and their loyalty can be called into question. This is why the ruling classes, with the keenest awareness of their own interests, are constantly on the lookout for, and wary of, any "collaborator" they deem unreliable. While they are generally reluctant to strike at this part of the social body, which ensures their legitimacy and longevity, they caved with the Gilets Jaunes. Rather Hitler than the Front Populaire! Rather

---

9   TN: "La loi du 24 août 2021 confortant le respect des principes de la République," also known as "loi contre le sépatisme" was passed by the French Parliament in 2021. The anti-separatism bill, aimed at "strengthening respect for the principles of the Republic" has been widely attacked as further institutionalizing State racism and Islamophobia. See, for instance, Yasser Louati, "France: Understanding the Roots of the Anti-Separatism Bill," *Islamic Human Rights Commission, The Long View* 4, no. 1 (January 2002): 3–8.

10   TN: "The Adama Generation," a mass mobilization and movement against anti-Black police violence and for racial justice that emerged in response to the death of Adama Traoré while in custody in 2016, after he had been brutalized and assaulted by police.

Zemmour than Mélenchon! That's the price many are willing to pay to nip any threat of dissent in the bud at a time when consensus is disintegrating and the democratic crisis is deepening. How else can we make sense of Zemmour if not as the last, panic-stricken resort of those in power, ready to do anything—including rehabilitate Pétain, whose very rejection was foundational to the Republican consensus—to lead the consciousness of Whites gone astray back into the fold of identitarian pride? Is this panic justified? Are the white working classes really so unreliable in their adherence to white power? Could they be betraying it? Is this a flaw in the armor, a breach through which to enter?

Highly doubtful. First, because working-class far-right voters are not mistaken in their anger. They vote out of conviction. So, it is inconceivable that they could all be transformed. As for the other popular parts of society, whether they vote or abstain, their critique of the political system rarely amounts to a disavowal of the imperialist nation. They register a complaint—against the failure to fulfill the promise of redistribution, the destruction of the welfare State and the rule of law—but never, or rarely, do they question the nature and conditions of existence that are ravaging the Global South.

Should we abandon all revolutionary alternatives? Give up hope of a fairer world? Is there room for such a thing as "optimism of the will"? If we follow certain Marxist analyses, the contradictions of capitalism are so untenable that they will inevitably lead to a socialist solution. Here again, we would have reason to doubt. Up until now, the ruling blocs have always managed to overcome these contradictions or come to terms with them. It is also possible to imagine endless rot. In short, optimism is not really on the agenda.

Yet this book would have no *raison d'être* if it had abandoned optimism. It would be shameful, in fact. We can only find our way back to optimism, however, if as activists we can identify that which, apart from their whiteness, characterizes the dignity of the French and, by extension, Europeans and Westerners. In other words, that which could divert them from their whiteness and grant them access to a new political imaginary. If this dignity proves to be a sufficiently powerful foundation, we may then imagine the outlines of a global strategy for breaking with the racial pact, an absolute precondition for any alliance between "rednecks" and "barbarians" and for a new political pact that could unite the working classes into what could also be called a "historical bloc" or a "decolonial majority."

This is a wager, one that can't be won in advance. But no wager is ever won in advance.

PART II

Revolutionary Love,
or Optimism of the Will

Do Whites Love Children?

A people is not just a calculating machine. Its fate cannot be treated simply as a business matter. A people is a collective being endowed with passions, emotions, and repulsions, with hopes and despairs, and the role of politicians deserving of the title, who do not treat it only as a job, is to interpret all of this and put it into a form that can be understood by the masses.[1]

—Jean-Marie Le Pen

ASIDE

One day, as I was leaving a debate I had been invited to participate in, I was challenged by a white leftist in her forties. She could hardly conceal her anger and spoke in a febrile voice. Here is my recollection of our brief exchange:

Her: "Madame Bouteldja, you're known to us, and we know you don't give a damn about the plight of homosexuals. That's your right, I guess, but there's one question you can't escape with your morality intact. And it has to do with our children. You can be against gay rights, you can hold forth about homosexuality as a Western phenomenon,[2] but the fact is that there are children at stake. Do you know what a child with two moms or two dads has to endure? Do you know what it's like for an eight-year-old to have to put up with the jeering and mockery of their classmates? I resent you for that, and I want you to know it!

The children. The sledgehammer argument had been released.

---

1 Jean-Marie Le Pen, in the documentary *Returning to Reims (Fragments)*, directed by Jean-Gabriel Périot (2021).
2 I never said this.

Me: "May I ask you a question?"

Her: "Yes."

Me: "Do you know if there are children in Mali?"

She looked at me, taken aback.

I repeated my question: "Do you know if there are children in Mali?"

Her: "I don't understand what you mean by this question. Of course there are children in Mali."

Me: "You claim to know that there are children in Mali, but I don't think you do. You don't know if there are children in Mali or not. Because, you see, I've been watching you for many months, you, the France that claims to love its children. I have been watching the confrontation between two white Frances unfold during the debate on equal marriage: conservative France vs. progressive France, right-wing and far-right France vs. left-wing and far-left France, reactionary France vs. humanist France. You, Ma'am, identify with humanist France. I've seen France mobilize powerful energies and affects, fervor, and faith on both sides … ."

Indeed, it was rather impressive, because for both of these Frances, something deeply ethical was playing out, especially around the question of children. But let me continue.

Me: "… This lasted several months. But did you know that François Hollande declared war on Mali precisely during this time?"

Her: "I don't recall."

Me: "I do. And do you know why? Because *I know* that there are children in Mali. And do you know how many marches the left organized to condemn this war?

None.

You didn't know this either, because the left you belong to—the left that loves its children, just as the right does—doesn't know that there are children in Mali. Because if it did, it would be outraged. And it would *also* be outraged for those children who were killed or orphaned by all the dirty French wars. So, when you claim to know that there are children in Mali, you're lying. I'm telling you something you don't know. I'm just like you. You don't know that there are children in Mali, just like I don't know that you have children. How could I be worried about them when I don't even know they exist?"

*   *   *

THE "PETTY WHITE," AN INTIMATE ENEMY

The real is when we clash. The reality, for petty Whites, is that they are despised. They're "*beaufs.*" Don't take it from me, take it from Cabu, who coined the word:

> The *beauf* is the guy who tells it like it is; he doesn't think at all, he's driven by commonplaces, by quote unquote "common sense," by certainties from which he will never budge. He doesn't read anymore. He doesn't read the newspapers. It's the death of paper.[3]

Paris holds the *beauf* in contempt. Cabu made the move to Paris. Cabu despises the *beaufs*. But I don't need him to convince me that they are despised. Nor do I need Paris. It's a personal feeling. I experience their social downgrading as an injustice, an anomaly, a personal affront, almost as a wound. I attribute this to my colonized-person neurosis, and to what remains of the lackey deep down inside. Like that day when, with an indigenous friend from the neighborhood, we ordered food and the delivery guy was a young white angel. Had he been Black or Arab, we wouldn't have thought twice about it, salam, salam. But that day, in the heat of the moment, we stopped him in his tracks, overcome by a feeling of guilt. "Wait up, here's five

---

3   Cabu, on the air with Gérard Holtz, November 10, 1979. TN: The French cartoonist first developed the figure of the *beauf* in the pages of the magazine, *Charlie Hebdo* (from 1973 to 1975) and later in the newspaper, *Le Canard Enchaîné*. The term, which stems from the word *beau-frère* (brother-in-law), is slang for "average reactionary Frenchperson," and entered the dictionary in 1985. For a useful overview of the origins of the term, see Pia Pandelakis, "The Cinematic Destiny of the French *Beauf*: National Shame or Hero?" *French Cultural Studies* 28, no. 3 (2017): 248–58.

bucks." We looked at each other: *meskin*.[4] Same feeling toward the petty Whites who never left the neighborhood, who were forced to live with us, as punishment. It's a feeling that is shared by many of the indigenous in the *cités*[5]—feeling bad for these white people who can't get out, who are tethered to the projects like a goat to a stake. And on top of that, they have to put up with our customs, or else imitate us, become us, to make up for their cumbersome—white—difference. Same thing with the Gilets Jaunes. If people were more interested in what the indigenous have to say, they would know that we know better than the experts at BFM[6] and all those chatty commentators. We know better than the left, which is always one diagnosis behind. We're ahead of the game, even, as is often the case.

The working-class indigenous instinct is never wrong. White people's fall from grace is a sorry sight, but it is the "quality" of this feeling that I'd like to focus on. It emerges in total opposition to the petty Whites' own fall from grace. There was something like a difference in nature between the reaction of petty Whites when the riots broke out in the *banlieues*[7] in 2005 and the reaction of the

---

4   Slang for "poor guy."
5   TN: "Structures which are often, but not always, found in banlieues and quartiers populaires. They are made up of towers and slabs of varying sizes, sometimes with insular passageways, and are generally closed in on themselves. This architecture, called 'grands ensembles,' was first experimented with in the former colonies ... before being introduced to metropolitan France." Mathieu Rigouste, "Quartiers Populaires and Banlieues: The Spatial Lexicon of French Structural Racism," trans. Chanelle Adams, *The Funambulist*, no. 50 (October 2023), last accessed June 11, 2024, https://thefunambulist.net/magazine/redefining-our-terms/quartiers-populaires-and-banlieues.
6   TN: BFM is a French news broadcast television and radio network.
7   TN: "While banlieue often refers to the outskirts of large cities, it can also describe places with large urban centers or the margins of small and medium-sized rural towns ... . Concentrating workers from regions far from major centers of accumulation, nearby countries, former colonies and all of the world, banlieues are produced and reproduced by regimes of socio-racial segregation." Rigouste, "Quartiers Populaires and Banlieues." Like *cité*, I have left these terms untranslated to gesture, as *The Funambulist* and translator Chanelle Adams have, to the loss of meaning that would result from translating this term or aligning it with the bourgeois conception of the "suburb."

indigenous during the Gilets Jaunes insurrection. This difference is best described by Maadou Killtran:

> The gilets jaunes asking Black people and Arabs to come help them is the best joke of 2018!!
>
> Wesh,[8] there's no work in the cités, no future, we grow up on top of each other all year round, we get heavier sentences than pedophiles for minor offenses, the schools are zoos, we could die or get nabbed during a simple ID check ... AND NOBODY GIVES A FUCK!!!!!!
>
> Not to mention the fact that there's probably a whole bunch of bastards in the gilets jaunes who'd just like to see us "go home" .... .
>
> You spit on us, the racaille,[9] wesh, you sign your kids up for pony classes so they don't cross paths with us at soccer, and now we're supposed to show up for you???? Lay off the crack.
>
> WE support, but we know that in court, a gilet jaune who works at Tourcoing and a guy from the 93[10] are going to get served different committal orders.
>
> Shut down the stock exchange, fuck up the Eiffel Tower, ransack the Place Vendôme, do what you like, but don't think for a second that we'll be your cannon fodder.
>
> Even though I left my cité a long time ago, I'm still a banlieusard at heart, and to see that you only want us because you can't stir shit up on your own is total bullshit.
>
> To all the guys from the cité, don't do it, hit up a deal, now's the time, we don't give a fuck about minimum wage.[11]

Maadou Killtran's prose hits the nail on the head and speaks volumes about the different conditions each faces. But what matters most here are these two, miraculous words: "We support."

---

8   TN: Slang derived from Arabic used as a greeting (akin to "yo") that similarly doubles as an interjection or emphasis.

9   TN: Derogatory term that may translate to "scum," "rabble," or other spiteful variants, used to refer, usually, to Arab or Black youth living in the banlieues or city centers.

10   TN: The 93 department in France, Seine-Saint-Denis.

11   Maadou Kiltran, Facebook post, November 2018.

During the 2005 riots in the *quartiers*,[12] petty Whites were, at best, indifferent, and at worst, eager for the cops to put an end to the *racailles*, the rioters, the disorder. There was no compassion to be found. The *quartiers*, however, had a completely different kind of attitude toward the Gilets Jaunes, a more diffuse feeling that had little to do with hostility. There was understanding and even a vexed solidarity, mixed with a desire for revenge and perhaps even a kind of perverse pleasure ("so what's it like to be put down[13] by the cops?"), and finally, a refusal to be part of it ("we're not infantrymen," "we're the ones they'll accuse of rioting"). But never any hostility. If you're not convinced, I invite you to reread Killtran's post. I'll carry on.

FACTS. In order to conceive of an alliance, however romanticized, between "rednecks" and "barbarians," we need to face the facts and consider this asymmetry of affects. FACTS. What can we expect from petty Whites—those strange strangers, vague relatives but not really cousins—and how can they be included within a global deco-lonial strategy when so little in their sensibility lends itself to this kind of rapprochement, but also when we refuse, on the indigenous side, to serve as mere infantrymen? The Gilets Jaunes and, more generally, the petty Whites, are a real headache for anyone envi-sioning the unity of the working classes as a strategic horizon. But because politics have little use for the empathy or generosity of one group toward another, I'll save this discordance for later.

For the moment, I'll embark on my raft—Killtran's two sublime words—to sail toward them, the petty Whites, from my indigenous perspective, and based on what I know or think I know about them.

"I HATE THOSE WHO ARE INDIFFERENT"

The French Revolution nearly produced a humanity that loves *all* children. Instead, it produced a humanity that loves *only* its children. And yet, in his remarkable book, *La démence coloniale sous Napoléon* [Colonial madness under Napoleon], Yves Benot—evoking the

---

12 TN: Most literally, "neighborhood," or *quartiers populaires*. See Rigouste, "Quartiers Populaires an Banlieues."

13 In French, *se faire haggar*, or "to be humiliated."

moment before Bonaparte reestablished slavery—explains that police reports from the time showed that French public opinion was not at all in favor of the emperor's imperial policy. It was first and foremost a matter for the owning classes:

> It goes without saying that colonial madness of the First Consul and the emperor was also that of an entire group of former colonists, civil servants, holdovers from the Ancien Régime, arms dealers, and of certain ministers, generals, and admirals.[14]

As a result, the first public decision on colonial matters after the *coup d'état* of 18 Brumaire was very cautious. The Consuls' proclamation of December 25, 1799, addressed to the "Brave blacks of Saint Domingo," promised to uphold the decree of 16 Pluviôse (or February 4, 1794), through which the Convention had abolished slavery. Bonaparte's hesitation can obviously be attributed to the Haitian Revolution, but it is also because of French public opinion, which was politically and subjectively shaped by the Revolution (and the 1793 Declaration of the Rights of Man). Slavery was nevertheless reestablished in 1802, but before this could happen, a rather recalcitrant public opinion had to be primed, and the principle of abolition reconciled, in practice, with its negation. Benot ponders:

> The most remarkable thing is that one wonders who the proclamation was really intended for; indeed, it was immediately published in the Parisian dailies, whereas, of course, neither Toussaint nor the "brave blacks" would come to know of it for several weeks … Was it not intended to provide immediate reassurance to the French public opinion, which was still congratulating itself on the decree of 16 Pluviôse?[15]

Here we can see the key features of the divide outlined by the Valladolid debate. It would be naive to believe that French public opinion was radically anti-colonialist and consistent in these senti-

14 Yves Benot, *La Démence coloniale sous Napoléon* (Paris: La Découverte, 2007), 10.
15 Ibid., 21.

ments, but we do know that popular sentiment favored anti-slavery, and that the ideals of the French Revolution, however unrealized, informed the fraternal humanism of the lower classes. This sentiment continued to irrigate the Paris Commune, albeit imperfectly. The conviction that one belonged to one and the same humanity was not taken as a given, yet here we can see the ideological foundation that would serve as ferment for the Third International, and later, the far left. At the same time, the institution of the nation-state was operative. The "person of French stock" supplanted the traditional, land-bound peasant, just as they supplanted the proletariat. The history of the abandonment of internationalist ideals is neither linear nor unequivocal, but the strong strands of chauvinism running through it are undeniable.

Today, the imperialist consensus is widespread. This consensus, which favors French interventions justified by the civilizing mission, and for the last twenty years, by the war on terror, has produced indifference to the horrors of war within public opinion and strengthened support for the idea that France should assume the role of a world power.

What is important in this brief historical reminder is that the ancestors of the Gilets Jaunes were already *othered*—and, to be honest, they weren't very white. In the past, Bonaparte had feared popular opinion when he set out to colonize—to the point of having to use subterfuges to achieve his ends. But the imperialist actions of Mitterrand in Iraq, Chirac in Afghanistan, Sarkozy in Libya, Hollande in Mali, and Macron in the Sahel provoked indifference, if not outright approval.

And yet.

Between 50 and 55 million people have died around the world as a result of Western colonialism and neo-colonialism since the end of World War II. This relatively short period has arguably seen the greatest number of massacres in human history.[16]

---

16 Andre Vltchek, "The Murderous Legacy of Colonialism," in Noam Chomsky and Andre Vltchek, *On Western Terrorism: From Hiroshima to Drone Warfare* (London: Pluto Press, 2017), 1.

55 million people.

What is the future Gilet Jaune thinking in 2013, when he learns, seated in front of his TV, that Hollande has decided to send troops to Mali? We could give him the benefit of the doubt and imagine that he felt troubled by a feeling of injustice and incomprehension. But will the informed activist be convinced by this generous hypothesis? For nothing in the revolt that would set France ablaze a few years later left even the slightest doubt as to the sedimented indifference of this category of the French population. With the exception of a few rare moments of epiphany, France's geopolitics were never mentioned, still less the question of war or the death industry. It is this *cultural* indifference to the plight of peoples martyred by our State, our weapons, and our multinationals that is most disturbing, most infuriating, and that makes the prospect of a major shift in white consciousness so difficult to imagine. Decolonialists are wont to say that the peoples of the Global South are not asking for repentance or apologies. It is to the people of France that the colonial powers should apologize, for having corrupted and enlisted them into the crime of colonization.

But are the French demanding such an apology from their representatives?

The question is pointless. They're too *innocent* for that.

We're told that the poor, being poor, have an excuse. They have other fish to fry. The poor are too bogged down in their day-to-day problems to worry about the fate of the wider world. Yet this argument has long since been dismantled by the less naive: "The citizens of the metropolis must be given the feeling that they are proprietors so they can hear the echoes of faraway gunfire without flinching."[17]

If those poor people are innocent, it's because they have a trait in common with their brothers in nationality: indifference. For indif-

---

17 "Don't visit the colonial exhibition," signed by André Breton, Paul Éluard, Benjamin Péret, Georges Sadoul, Pierre Unik, André Thirion, René Crevel, Aragon, René Char, Maxime Alexandre, Yves Tanguy, Georges Malkine, May 1931, reprinted in *Surrealism Against the Current: Tracts and Declarations*, ed. and trans. Michael Richardson and Krzysztof Fijałkowski (London: Pluto Press, 2001), 184–5.

ference is also a trait, a culture. They are indifferent to France the watchdog, France the *barbouze*,[18] France the bomber, France the meddler, France the beheader of regimes, because the relationship that France entertains with the world is normal. And the very nature of normality is to be normal. Unquestionable. As unquestionable as the rising or setting sun, as the clouds before the rain. The worst thing is to have a "soul deadened by habit," said Charles Péguy.[19] And yet, the fact of imagining that they can and should ask themselves questions should not be an insult to them.

Questions such as this one, for example, which is accessible to all: Would the French find it normal if they were bombed in the name of democracy? Would they find it normal for the Central African Armed Forces to patrol the streets of Toulouse, Paris, or Bordeaux, and impose their rule? Would they find it normal for foreign powers to choose their rulers in their place, to depose or kill their presidents? The answer is so obvious that the question is never raised. And yet do "rednecks," as despicable as they may seem to the eyes of Parisian parvenus, make use of their "common sense" to confront the obvious? Not quite. Indifference is a trait of white humanity, because every white person, no matter how poor, instinctively knows that this order benefits them. The poor or downtrodden— the petty Whites, the proles, the middle classes—are part of this order, and it is together with them, with a humanity that loves *only* its children, that we will have to come to a compromise.

---

18 TN: *Barbouze*, which translates to the "bearded ones" or the "fake-beards," refers to a group of French armed counterinsurgents and extra-judicial militias established with the purpose of suppressing and destabilizing the OAS in Algeria from 1961 to 1962.

19 TN: "There is something even worse than having a soul that is perverse. And that is to have a soul that is deadened by habit." This translation of Charles Péguy's "The Duration of a People: Descartes, Bergson, and Modern Philosophy" is given by Matthew Steven Gervase in "Towards a Republican Ethics of *Fraternité: Charles Péguy's Mystical Refashioning of Civic Virtue*," PhD diss.ertation (University of California, Santa Cruz, 2018), 241. See also: "Conjoined Note on Descartes and the Cartesian Philosophy," in *Notes on Bergson and Descartes: Philosophy, Christianity, and Modernity in Contestation*, trans. Bruce K. Ward (Eugene, OR: Cascade Books, 2019).

FACTS. Therein lies the heart of the problem. Therein lies the knot. Therein lies the wager.

PETTY WHITES, VICTIMS OF STATE ANTIRACISM

Soft ideology is an orgy. An ideological orgy between the left and the right. It was the dominant ideology of the '80s, which is to say the one that reconciled the beautiful souls with the good managers, and the right with the left, around a program of social conservatism, and of defense of institutions and the socio-economic system, which is cloaked in a discourse of moralism, humanitarianism, and antiracism. Right-wing management cloaked in left-wing rhetoric.[20]

The extent to which the sidelining of major ideological confrontations and the disappearance of workers' organizations have dislocated and scattered the proletarian classes cannot be overstated. But this history is relatively well known. Much less is known about the disastrous effects of State or moral antiracism (a subcategory of soft ideology) on the most precarious and vulnerable white populations.

One might consider that moral antiracism has been used as an ideological weapon to thwart all forms of political self-organizing by immigrant communities. And one would be right. One might also consider how it has been used to depoliticize struggles against discrimination and the police. Here too, one would be right. That it redirected anger against the State toward the Front National and the "rednecks." Nothing could be more true. However, it would be a mistake to underestimate the performative effects of this discourse, and the damage—both moral and material—it has caused to the petty Whites, who feel they have been wronged by this compromise, when the racial/national pact was supposed to give them priority. The idea that there exists an "elite" preference for non-Whites is a belief that fosters competition and resentment rather than conver-

---

20 François-Bernard Huygue, on the show "Bain de minuit," December 4, 1987.

gence. But instead of condemning this sentiment, I think it would be more constructive to distinguish between what is true and what is false in this complaint. Because there is, we must admit, some truth to it.

When the insurgent Gilets Jaunes burst onto the political scene, petty Whites from the peripheries and the countryside suddenly muddled a division whose most mediatized conflicts over the past forty years essentially pitted central power against the indigenous banlieues. Interlopers of sorts, the Gilets Jaunes stepped into this seemingly timeless face-off that conflates all other contradictions. Emerging from nowhere to reclaim their share of dignity on identitarian and social grounds, the Gilets Jaunes expressed, through their anarchic and disorganized words and actions, something similar to the African American slogan, "Black lives matter." In so doing, they claimed to be the *real* victims of the system. Even greater victims, in other words, than the ones favored by the ruling class, the elites, the entertainment industry, and the media. Even greater victims than non-Whites. They were the ones to have been truly neglected, truly left behind. This was enough to destabilize the politically defined indigenous individual, who considers the postcolonial subject to be the ultimate victim of the social order, and all Whites as superior in status.

Are petty Whites victims of the social, symbolic, and political order? If this question could have been raised before the Gilets Jaunes, after them, there can be no doubt about it. Not only because they affirmed it collectively—which should be enough to take them seriously—but also because we cannot forget that liberal democracies have never erased class divisions. They have merely rendered these divisions opaque through the development of the middle and upper classes. Beggars come in all shapes and sizes, and so too do the bourgeoisie and the ruling classes.

Petty Whites are well and truly victims. But before determining who of the indigenous or the petty White is the real victim, and before defining the strategic utility of this fact, it is important not to cast doubt on the feeling too many Whites harbor, namely, that not only are they despised as victims, but also that "it all goes to the *racailles* from the *banlieues*." Worse still, they would be denied the right to call themselves victims, since that position is already occupied. Let's pause here for a moment. France's political theater is so dominated by illusionists, magicians, and other manipulators that the temptation to agree wholeheartedly with this sentiment is strong—one must be well equipped to resist it. Let's begin by separating fact from fiction.

What the Gilets Jaunes are really saying is that there's been a betrayal. France has abandoned them; they have been dispossessed of the motherland that is theirs by blood. They are Gauls, France belongs to them by right—genetically one could argue— but it's slipping away from them because "the cosmopolitan elites" have decided otherwise, favoring the indigenous to them. Public authorities in major cities have abandoned them to come to the aid of "problem neighborhoods," spending the public money that is rightfully theirs. It is their hard work that finances urban policies, the rehabilitation of housing projects, and positive discrimination policies, yet they have become invisible; they are ignored, deprived of public services, schools, daycare, hospitals, post offices, train stations, and media attention. Not only are they taxed, but they also bear the brunt of rising costs of living as they tumble down the social ladder. And yet, it's the banlieue that gets all the support, even from a symbolic point of view. Because the banlieue isn't just a place of poverty, violence, and delinquency, it's also *sexy*. The banlieue fascinates the *bobos*,[21] high society, cinema, and fashion. The aesthetics of the banlieue shape good taste and what's trendy. What could the "hick" possibly have to offer next to indigenous swag? "Too white to interest the left, too poor to interest the right,"[22] says Aymeric Patrico, pointedly. When they revolt, they display their scorned dignity, and when this dignity manifests itself, its essence is often expressed in the form of the flag, the homeland, identity, and soil.

---

21 TN: A portmanteau word designating the socio-economic "bohemian-bourgeois" group in France.
22 Aymeric Patricot, *Les petits blancs: Un voyage dans la France d'en bas* (Paris: Editions Plein Jour, 2013).

Let's be honest. The Gilets Jaunes can't be put on trial for openly expressing racist sentiments or genuinely supporting far-right ideas. It's all very noteworthy, but surprising nonetheless. Why might this be the case?

Why didn't they open the sluice gates of their chauvinistic instincts even wider? Why such restraint? This question could be analyzed as the manifestation of an indigenous paranoia that sees racists everywhere.

Maybe so. In fact, they were nowhere near being as politically determined by the far right as true identitarian activists are.

But maybe not, because the Gilets Jaunes have an intimate knowledge. A kind of knowledge that's imperceptible at first glance because it has been tracked. They know elite France. They know they are constrained by the ideological apparatus of bourgeois righteousness. Nearly forty years of moral antiracism weigh on their shoulders. This antiracism may be decrepit, even moribund, but the spirit of Mitterrand, of Attali, of Canal+, and SOS Racisme is alive and well. Think of Mr. and Mrs. Dupont, with their narrow-minded and crude ideas (they love Bigard and Sébastien[23] and are always one ribald remark ahead), their dubious tastes (they listen to Johnny and Sardou[24]), and their racist, sexist, and homophobic prejudices. They are the ones who are put on blast when the far right surfaces. The ones who are accused of spitting on Arabs and getting a little trigger-happy at times. The ones who have to quiet their frustration when they feel they've been wronged by those less deserving than them; the ones who have to swallow their anger when they're reprimanded or assaulted at school by their indigenous "classmates." The ones who need to be taught a thing or two when they balk at marrying their daughter off to a Black man. The ones to whom the nice white guy's invective "Hands off my pal" is addressed.[25] The ones who pay the highest price for "antiracist" peacemaking policies ... since they are its main scapegoats. To put it plainly, public authorities have sys-

---

23 TN: Jean-Marie Bigard and Patrick Sébastien.
24 TN: Johnny Hallyday and Michel Sardou.
25 "Hands off my pal" is a translation of "Touche pas à mon pote," the official slogan of the French antiracist association, SOS Racisme, founded in 1984.

tematically shifted the blame for the French State's structural racism to the Front National/Rassemblement National and to the petty Whites, that is, to the safeguard of Republican racism and the lower rungs of the racial order, respectively. The latter find themselves having to swallow lies and "tolerate" their swarthy neighbors—a duty which, needless to say, is in no way imposed on champagne socialists, who know themselves exempt from this by virtue of the social gap separating them from the indigenous—while the indigenous scoff at them, anchored in their cultural omnipotence, their unwavering faith, their beauty, and their capacity for revolt. The indigenous who dare to ransack public buildings, to burn cars, free of all the rules of decorum imposed on decent folks. Those who get up early, work harder but earn less. To the unspoken "fuck you" on the tip of their tongues retorts the masterful, insolent, and flattening indigenous "motherfucker!" uttered with shocking disinhibition.

The subcontracting of racism to the white working classes has been accompanied by the muzzling of their frustration and resentment. Good conscience and its impulse to censor continue to police deviant souls. The lesson has been learned. Petty Whites know the beast that stands before them. In fact, all they have done is practice a kind of taqiyya.[26] In traffic circles, in Gilets Jaunes demonstrations, the racist sentiment was hushed. Not dominating, not crushing, but hushed. This is the case not only because the Gilets Jaunes' main demands were actually social and genuinely directed at the high cost of living, but also because their instinct was not to let their good conscience get the better of them. Let us not forget the antisemitic incident that cost them so much. They knew they'd be screwed if xenophobic tendencies took over, since the "elites" would band together with the banlieue and the Jews. They found the right, carefully considered punchline: "Furious, but not fascist!"[27]

---

26   A practice from the Koran that enables believers to conceal their true beliefs. TN: "Taqiyya," Wikipedia, last modified June 6, 2024, last accessed June 11, 2024, https://en.wikipedia.org/wiki/Taqiyya.

27   TN: "Fâchés mais pas fachos!" is a near-homonymic play on words between "fâchés" (angry) and "fachos" (fascist) that is, unfortunately, not replicable in English.

So be it, but let's reconsider the complaint: "it all goes to the immigrants." Fact or fiction? How can we debunk this misconception when the media landscape is saturated with this idea? To blame: the March for Equality and Against Racism of 1983, which sounded the death knell of the good old days. Nothing would ever be the same again. The Barbarians are on our doorstep. This sent such a shockwave that it required a reaction in equal measure. Since then, lists have been endlessly drawn up of all the rehabilitation programs for so-called "problem" neighborhoods, programs with the stated goal of "reducing disparities in development in large urban housing projects in order to restore republican equality."[28] Money poured in … for urban policy and urban renewal, for security and delinquency prevention, for social development and the fight against unemployment. Are we to conclude that the indigenous banlieues have been favored over the white peripheries? This is what is argued by proponents of the theory of "peripheral France"[29]—a theory that proposes a new reading of territorial divisions. Rather than oppose immigrant cités to bourgeois centers, it opposes metropolises, including the banlieues, to the French peripheries and countryside. The former, according to this theory, would be the beneficiaries of globalization, the latter, its victims. We could give credence to such a hypothesis did it not turn working-class cities into the victors of happy globalization or create an affinity between banlieusards and bobos that is as imagined as it is implausible. Yet this is exactly what it does. And this is what the petty Whites so staunchly believe—indoctrinated as they are by their resentment, the media circus, and these kinds of nebulous theories that claim to listen to the people but are merely ethnicist and idiotically vindictive. Because, while it is true that the banlieues have benefited from charity, this has been less out of a concern for social justice than because of the dangerous proximity of the Barbarians to Civilization. Paris, Lyon, Bordeaux, Toulouse …

---

28   TN: "Politique de la ville," Agence Nationale de la Cohésion des Territoires, last accessed June 11, 2024, https://agence-cohesion-territoires.gouv.fr/politique-de-la-ville-97.

29   Christophe Guilluy, *La France périphérique: Comment on a sacrifié les classes populaires* (Paris: Flammarion, 2014).

The bourgeois heartland is just a few metro or RER stops away. The money that is spent, the budgets that are ratified, are not intended to enact justice. They buy social peace. Major bourgeois centers and their authorized representatives have one obsession: control over the indigenous populace. And one major task to accomplish: to solve the Great Equation. Their domestic workers, upon whom their daily lives depend economically, must remain within a stone's throw, like the squires on their estates. Servants, maids, grooms, gardeners, and nannies are housed in the attic or the basement, out of sight but close at hand. Christophe Guilluy can wax lyrical about the fantasy of a privileged banlieue, but his theorizing does not stand up to any materialist analysis. As its name suggests, the standard of living of France's lowest class is below that of France's lower class. With all due respect, immigrant neighborhoods are generally, and by far, the poorest in France. The money that buys social peace is counter-revolutionary. This manna keeps the indigenous in line. Cronyism buys everything, even revolt. The indigenous tend to be the poorest— the last to be hired, the first to get fired—and they do not have the same political and social rights as others. They do not have the right to organize outside the control of the State. Their beliefs are criminalized, their places of worship under pressure. What is sacred to them gets trampled on. The indigenous fill prisons. They die at the hands of police bullets and generally have no right to a fair trial. Anything can be said about them, and with total impunity; they can be dragged through the mud and accused of anything. Finally, they are accountable for any crime committed by one of their fellow men, from the most minor news item to the attacks at the Bataclan. In short, one wonders what they're doing here, and dreams of getting rid of them … except, they can always be useful when it comes to revitalizing the working class in the areas it finds itself most lacking, in the places petty Whites definitely don't want to be: the indigenous were on the frontlines during the Covid-19 pandemic, for instance. However, since the crash of 2008, petty Whites have been dropping out. They aren't as poor as the indigenous, but they're getting dangerously close. All the warning signs are flashing; many have crossed the poverty line. Hundreds of thousands, perhaps even millions, are becoming indigenized. This social and statutory disengagement can be seen as either a political threat or a godsend. And both are the case in some places, so strong is the appeal of the far right, and so vivid the memory of social and trade union struggles past. We're walking on a razor's edge.

Official antiracism and the instrumentalization of the Front National were two sides of the same deliberate and resolute State policy. The aim was to reaffirm the power bloc's hegemony by keeping two groups in check: the petty Whites, whom the liberal government was preparing to betray, and the indigenous, whose agitation raised fears of a radicalization of social struggles. Thus, the moral antiracism that spread widely during the 1980s was nothing but an update of the racial pact, shaped by the desire for equality of descendants of postcolonial immigrants, and the need for the State (with the support of the institutional left and part of the radical left) to guarantee and perpetuate racial privilege, without which it risked losing the approval of the white masses. This strategy had paradoxical effects. On the one hand, petty Whites had to be taught a lesson in antiracism, while immigrants had to learn about Republican integration. On the other, Whites had to be reassured by pandering to the far right ("France cannot welcome all the misery in the world,"[30] or "The Front National is asking the right questions, but giving the wrong answers"). Pursued by the formerly colonized and the restless Global South, the racial pact has continued to adapt over time, and with every passing decade more ground is ceded to the far right. It can therefore be asserted that those in power have deliberately increased the level of racism among Whites and used it as an adjustment variable, whereas any social policies capable of reducing it were rendered inoperative by the revitalized dynamism of liberalism and the historic capitulation of the left—a capitulation that, as we have seen, was strongly defined by its substantive whiteness.

---

30 TN: CRS, quoted in Jasmine Moody, "'We Cannot Welcome All the Misery in the World': Fewer Migrants Stopped by French Authorities in 2023 than 2022," *BBC News*, September 12, 2023, last accessed June 11, 2024, www.lbc.co.uk/news/fewer-migrants-stopped-by-french-authorities-2023-than-2022-channel-france-uk/.

CREDIT TO SORAL WHERE CREDIT IS DUE

Alain Soral deserves credit for having been able to touch the souls of two groups with opposing interests at once, and for having been the first to conceive of a politics of rednecks and barbarians. He was the first to see it. The first to sense it. The first to have theorized and then developed a counter-intuitive idea: to make the hearts and minds of the most despised, yet antagonistic, categories of society vibrate in unison. His large audience was essentially made up of Black people, Arabs, and petty Whites. Men, more specifically. Young. Poor. Those who are without a homeland—some because they are excluded from it, others because it has betrayed them—found in his argument the articulation of their existential malaise. Soral offered up a nation-alistic, masculinist, and antisemitic discourse—each of these three axes striking at the heart of the unrest experienced, differentially, by these two sections of the population.

While the stateless indigenous suffers from being nowhere at home—he has left one country without finding another—Soral, unlike the rest of the white political field, finally gives him the opportunity to belong to a national entity, endowed with History and Power: France. Soral understood that the indigenous in need of a homeland has sincere, frustrated feelings toward France, like a spurned lover who fantasizes about "fucking her until she loves him."[31] Soral goes one step further. He tells the indigenous to stay true to himself, to claim his culture, to claim his Muslim faith ... on the condition that it be subordinated to the national interest. This proposal contradicts ideas of transnational Ummah or Pan-Africanism, but it corresponds to the requirements of Republican integration. Half a loaf is better than none. The indigenous is used to it. For the petty Whites, Soral serves up a conspiratorial, antisemitic, and anti-globalization discourse. French pride would seem to be the last resort against the disorder of capitalism—a nationalistic pride

---

31 TN: Adapted from a line in French rapper BEN plg's 2022 song "Jusqu'à ce qu'elle s'aime," track 11 on the album *Réalité Rap Musique*, vol. 2, Pour La Gloire 538871352, CD, 2022. In French, the original lyric is "on va baiser la France jusqu'à ce qu'elle s'aime" (We're going to fuck France until it loves itself).

for which the indigenous have a certain empathy. After all, they were the first to brandish the Algerian flag, to flaunt their Africanness. Why deny "true Frenchpeople" what they have forcibly claimed for themselves? As for the antisemitic aspect of the argument, it is met with approval, since Jews are perceived by both petty Whites and the indigenous as favorites and privileged. Favorites, because the nationalism that produced them has always been antisemitic, and privileged because, as legitimists, they compete with a group rightly perceived as non-white. The preference (which we prefer to call philosemitism) to which the Jewish community is subjected in spite of itself, is perceived as a profound injustice. But it's a godsend for Soral. Finally, most of them are men. Men suffocated by an inhibited masculinity, but men nonetheless—white and indigenous men violently attached to their virility. This is surely the most sensitive issue, and the first to draw the attention of indigenous men to Soral back in 2004, on Thierry Ardisson's show, *Tout le monde en parle* [The talk of the town]. The polemicist's appearance caused a stir and became a TV reference for many young men in the *quartiers*. Halfway through a long stream of verbal diarrhea, he evoked these masculinities sidelined by the power of hegemonic white masculinity, and offered a few insights that struck a chord with indigenous men:

There's always a possibility for the pretty "beurette,"[32] like the famous "l'Aziza," to leave the banlieue by flaunting her ass in night clubs that the guy can't get into. Let's not underestimate the pain that the Franco-Maghrebi man feels, standing outside of a building that his sister has been invited into, while he has only his poverty to offer. Let's not forget that, when you're a guy and you want to invite a girl out to dinner, contrary to all that feminist bullshit, you have to pay for yourself and for the girl, because it's a competition between males. You have to make twice as much money, but guys make half as much.

---

32 TN: A term drawing from the French slang *verlan* for Arab young woman.

In just a few words, Soral described a real social malaise that was unanimously silenced as Ni Putes Ni Soumises[33] reached the height of its media fame. His argument, in a nutshell: the "rascal" is deprived of any social status, since he does not have a job and can no longer even play his historical role as head of the family; this hardship is not compensated for by any other kind of sociability; State ideologies made him compete against the women in his community, so his sisters have become both vectors of his humiliation and trophies in the hands of white men. Earlier in the debate, Soral denounced the equation Muslims = gang rapists. He hit the nail on the head.

The male malaise among petty Whites is no less intense, and just as urgent to address. First, because white masculinity is based on an imperative of domination that today is being thwarted by the global decline of the West. France's decline is also a crisis of French masculinity. Second, because unlike for the white upper classes, the loss of this masculine power has not been met by any form of social compensation that would be as satisfying as masculine dignity. For them, masculinity is a guarantee of advancement, dignity, and strength in a world where the values they hold dear are going up in flames. As Olivier Schwartz shows:

> The canons of virility and masculinity can only be reconsidered if individuals can exchange them for other socially legitimate modes of being: this is precisely what is not so obvious within working-class categories.[34]

... and Pierre Bourdieu:

> I try to explain the attachment to the values of masculinity, physical strength, by pointing out, for example, that it's characteristic of people who have little to fall back on except their labour power, and sometimes their fighting strength. I try to show in

---

33   TN: Ni Putes Ni Soumises (Neither Whores Nor Submissive) is a French feminist movement founded in 2002 that combats violence targeting women.
34   Olivier Schwartz, *Le monde privé des ouvriers: Hommes et femmes du nord* (Paris: Quadrige/PUF, 2009), 206.

what respect the relationship to the body that is characteristic of the working class is the basis for a whole set of attitudes, behaviours and values, and that it is the key to understanding their way of talking or laughing, eating or walking. I say that the idea of masculinity is one of the last refuges of the identity of the dominated classes.[35]

Masculinity is also a resource for confronting this shadow war waged against the subaltern classes: "To man up" as a way of responding to the humiliations of the working class; of rehabilitating oneself in one's own eyes and in the eyes of one's family, wife, and children; and of facing a disturbing world wherein sociabilities are scattered.

White men from the working classes and indigenous men do belong to the capitalist and heterosexist world; they participate in it but do not inhabit it in the same way as the upper classes, who reap the maximum dividend. They suffer separately from the same evil: They must assume the mandate of masculinity that is imposed on them in every heterosexist society and this produces a hatred of the "emasculated" among women of their respective groups, thus adding to the pressure they experience. They continue to uphold this mandate for want of an alternative that could liberate them from it. For, if this alternative exists, only men of the upper classes enjoy it, shedding the seemingly crudest attributes of masculinity to lead a more refined life, thus ensuring their *distinction*. A distinction that will persist as long as they can subcontract their masculinity to an imperialist, belligerent State that will do the job for them. So, as I was saying, petty white and indigenous males suffer separately from the same evil, but they are themselves in competition: white men against indigenous men, vying for an honor that only the most disastrous (far-right or jihadist) ideologies can attain given the lack of political clairvoyance on the part of a left that struggles to reach them, caught up as it is in an abstract, out of touch progressivism. Should we blame the left for this, when we know how explosive the

35 Pierre Bourdieu, *Sociology in Question*, trans. Richard Nice (London: Sage, 1993), 20–1.

terrain is? On the one hand, white men are terrified of losing "the white woman" to indigenous men (which would be experienced as a national affront, since their consciousness tells them that they occupy the upper rungs of the hierarchy of peoples); on the other, indigenous men are terrified of losing "the indigenous woman" to the white competitor (which would confirm that they are indeed at the bottom of the basket of empire). Should we blame the left, when the women's insurrection unleashed by the #MeToo movement imposed a feminist agenda that is as imperative and urgent as it is blind to the contradictions of patriarchy and the need for a clear-sighted feminist strategy to target the main enemy?

In April 2022, during the presidential election, the inhabitants of the *quartiers* sprung a surprise when many of them took to the polls to vote for Mélenchon, who had understood how to speak to their hearts and souls during the campaign. They did this even as a large portion of the Gilets Jaunes, and more broadly of the white working classes, voted for the Rassemblement National—the only political party to maintain an affective relationship with the lower classes—propelling the far-right party into the second round of the presidential election for the third time during the Fifth Republic. The former wanted their share of the nation, the latter claimed its exclusivity.

FACTS.

THE BLUES OF THE OPTIMISTIC INDIGENOUS

There's an ocean of difference between petty Whites of the Gilet Jaune or Soralian variety, and a white person of the same kind as that lady who reproached me for not giving a shit about her children. The former stick out their tongue. The latter belong to the middle and upper classes that have not yet been affected by social down-grading. They don't socialize. But what they do have in common is their alienation from the nation of France. They depend upon it. They were integrated into it through the long history of workers' chauvinism, but also through its metamorphoses, which during this period would take the form, most recognizably, of femonationalism and homonationalism. We know how the proles can let themselves be tempted by the far right when resignation has not won out. We also know how women and homosexuals can drift to the right or the far right, provided they obtain certain reassurances. But what about this leftist lady who loves her children so much? Will she resist?

A gray veil passed over her face. Something resembling hatred, as in a moment of truth—the moment when you might fall to the dark side. I thought to myself that the border between left and right can be very porous when it comes to the indigenous, and that the veil that suddenly darkened this progressive woman's gaze could push her into the arms of the vile beast without warning and without her even realizing it. In all good conscience. After all, she does love her children.

Who is this woman? Is she just a "creature" of French history, a conjunctural being shaped by modernity, conflict, struggle, and the great compromises of history? Or something else? Could she be something else? I am neither a judge nor a prosecutor. Consequently, I can't and won't condemn her. On the contrary, I consider her. She EXISTS. There is, in her, the potential for a sister.

This is why I am mean to her. She prevents me from loving her children.

ASIDE

He was driving his car, when at a red light, another car pulled up next to his. The [white man] on the [passenger's side] recognized him. "Malcolm X!" he called out. He stuck his hand out of his car. "Do you mind shaking hands with a white man?" Just as the traffic light turned green, before hitting the gas, Malcolm replied: "I don't mind shaking hands with human beings. Are you one?"[36]

Reader, did you notice how the title of this chapter sounds like a distant echo of Malcolm's question?

Sad, don't you think?

---

36 Malcolm X, in *The Autobiography of Malcolm X: As Told to Alex Haley* (New York: Random House, 1965), 382. Cited in Sadri Khiari, *Malcolm X: Stratège de la dignité noire* (Paris: Amsterdam, 2012), 99. TN: The entire paragraph is largely citing Malcom X's first-person recollection, though it has been paraphrased and abridged here. The full quote is gestured to in brackets.

Dirty Hands

My second concern has to do with the actions of a disturbed person, an extremist, who might go shoot up a mosque or attack women wearing the veil; if such an event were to occur or be repeated several times, we would lose the moral advantage we have gained as a nation that has fallen victim to Islamist terrorism.[1]
—Pascal Bruckner, after the assassination of Samuel Paty

ASIDE

I let myself be told that my talk entitled "Les Beaufs et les Barbares, sortir du dilemme" ["Rednecks and Barbarians: Exiting the Dilemma"],[2] presented at the Bandung of the North conference a few months before the Gilets Jaunes insurrection, had struck a chord with the radical left. I had tried to explain that white and non-white workers weren't "clean," that they were pretty reactionary, actually, and that we would just have to deal with it. Not that we should encourage them in this direction or urge them to come together through militant demagoguery, but that we should try to look for the bright side. As politically indigenous people having to face our own corruption, it's our duty to keep asking ourselves Baldwin's question: "What will happen to all of that beauty?" And when you're white, to respond to another kind of torment as honestly as possible:

It seems easy to convince yourself in the abstract that you will never speak to anyone who votes for the Front National, never

---

1 Pascal Bruckner, "The grand féminisme, dans lequel j'ai été élevé, était un féminisme de réconciliation," *France Inter*, October 22, 2020.
2 Houria Bouteldja, "Les Beaufs et les Barbares: sortir du dilemne," Parti des Indigènes de la République, June 21, 2018. TN: The "Bandung du Nord: Vers une Internationale Décoloniale" (Bandung of the North: Toward a Decolonial International) conference took place at the Bourse du travail de Saint-Denis on May 4–6, 2018, last accessed June 11, 2024, https://bandungdunord.webflow.io/.

shake their hand. But how do you react when you discover that these people are part of your own family? What do you say? What do you do? What do you think?[3]

In the end, what had I said that my illustrious predecessors had not?

Whoever expects a "pure" social revolution will *never* live to see it. Such a person pays lip-service to revolution without understanding what revolution is.[4]

The text had circulated. The white left like it. This delighted me and restored my hope because, at its core, my argument wasn't so much that we should take into consideration the negative affects of the lower classes, but that we should grasp their practical consequences: we need to agree to getting our *hands dirty*.

*   *   *

A proverb—a Chinese one, it would appear—goes as follows: "Once a word leaves your mouth, you cannot chase it back even with the swiftest horse."

The word "Israeli" no longer belonged to Miss Provence the moment she uttered it, on that December day in 2020.[5] It belonged to the world. Had France been only a country of White people—people who love their children—there would have been no Miss Provence controversy. But it is also made up of the indigenous—people who still love other people's children a little—and their reaction reflected the moral decay and great schizophrenia of our time:

---

3 See *Retour à Reims*, directed by Jean-Gabriel Périot. TN: Didier Eribon, *Returning to Reims*, trans. Michael Lucey (Los Angeles: Semiotext(e), 2013), 115.
4 Vladimir Lenin, "The Discussion on Self-Determination Summed up" (1916), last accessed June 11, 2024, www.marxists.org/archive/lenin/works/1916/jul/x01.htm.
5 During the 2021 Miss France pageant, Miss Provence [April Benayoum] mentioned her father's Israeli nationality, sparking controversy on social media.

"Uncle Hitler, you forgot to exterminate Miss Provence"—the antisemitic tweet.

"Miss Provence is Israeli, get her out of here."—the anti-Zionist tweet.

The dark side, the bright side. The media had already voted for the dark side. Barbarians! Barbarians! The left was silent. Out of cowardice, out of conviction, out of indifference. Because words, *that word*, has no effect on them. The left loves its children, but above all, it wants to keep its hands clean, white, and immaculate; it does not want to take any risks, only continue to gaze at its own reflection. It wants the indigenous to join its protests and its organizations without having to lift a finger. The left doesn't even contemplate ways to recruit them. It doesn't want to give anything in return. And above all, it loathes getting dirty. And with the indigenous, you get dirty. A little. A lot. It's unavoidable.

I, among the Barbarians, had heard it. As soon as *the word* came out of the ingenue's mouth, it belonged to all of us, and I started receiving all the text messages circulating among the indigenous. "What? An Israeli!!! No way we're voting for her!"

But the media had taken sides, and everyone had fallen silent, even and especially those on the left who purported to *understand* "Beaufs et Barbares." The left that is always ready to pull the pin on a grenade, but suspends the act just at the fateful moment, for fear of damaging the red nail polish on its manicured fingers. The left that, once again, had given the right and the far right the exclusive license to define the indigenous. Barbarians. Period. And nothing more. Certainly not people who, in their great "disorientation" as Badiou would say, still know how to love other people's children.

And I, alas, had written about this. Could I retract my statement? I had said that commitment is impure, that you have to know how to get your hands dirty, to plunge into the shit. That you can't be involved in politics without getting splashed. If I said nothing, how could I show face. And then what? Give Bruckner the moral high ground? I'd rather dive straight into the muck than let people think we've become soulless.

So I spoke out.[6] I was buried in shit. Called an "antisemite." Then dropped by (almost)[7] everyone—all those who want to keep their hands clean but never use them for anything.

DIRTY HANDS AND THE MORAL ADVANTAGE

He's a despicable figure—this is well established since the publication of *The Tears of the White Man*,[8] but even more so since he hypocritically disowned his Nazi-collaborator father and offered up that chilling definition of "moral advantage," which draws its lifeblood from the victims of terrorism. And yet, we can't accuse Pascal Bruckner of lacking strategic vision. His cynicism is matched only by his keen understanding of the interests of the class-race he represents. And if the decolonial and antiracist camp also had some strategic ambitions, it would first have to recognize that Bruckner's "concern," however obscene, is based on an accurate, if sinister, premise. Indeed, we saw how the murder of Samuel Paty[9] was immediately seized upon as a "moral advantage"; how it enabled the government, confronted with a stunned public opinion, to impose a racist and liberticide security agenda. The least we can say is that our leaders knew how to brilliantly and opportunistically make the most of the situation. We must remember the sequence of events that preceded this brutal takeover to understand the ruling classes'

6 Houria Bouteldja, "L'anti-tatarisme des Palestiniens (et des banlieues) n'existe pas—À propos de Miss Provence et de l'antisémisme (le vrai)," *UJFP*, December 26, 2020.

7 "Contre la calomnie et la diffamation, en soutien à Houria Bouteldja," Acta. zone, January 17, 2021, last accessed June 11, 2024, https://acta.zone/contre-la-calomnie-et-la-diffamation-en-soutien-a-houria-bouteldja/.

8 TN: Pascal Bruckner, *Le Sanglot de l'homme blanc* (Paris: Éditions du Seuil, 1983) was translated into English by William R. Beer and published by Free Press (New York) in 1986.

9 TN: Elementary school teacher in Éragny-sur-Oise killed and beheaded in October 2020 after showing his students *Charlie Hebdo* caricatures of the Prophet Muhammad in a class on free speech. The six teenagers convicted for his murder in 2023 have been variously called "Islamist extremists" and "Islamist militants" in a case that launched widespread debate about freedom of speech, integration, and Islamophobia in France.

outburst and their determination. Since the end of the Hollande quinquennium, the Valls, Philippe, and Castex governments have had to face, in succession, the anger of social unrest, the Nuit Debout movement,[10] the Gilets Jaunes, the Black Bloc, the railworkers' strike, and the growing struggle against Islamophobia and the police State. It would be a big mistake to underestimate the terror of the ruling classes which, in truth, are the only ones who can really claim a genuine organized and structured class consciousness. They may have to put up with a few peasant revolts here and there, but they will certainly not endure the long-term establishment of an insurrection that even remotely resembles a unification of white and non-white working classes or suggests the distant possibility of revolution. Consequently, they pull out all the stops.

Bruckner may not be wrong, then, to regard every jihadist attack, whether it has been claimed as such or not, as a godsend. In fact, the period that followed was one of total excess, starting with the so-called "global security" bill.[11] While the bill provoked genuine indignation and mobilization, this quickly faded when the government played its Islamophobic card: the separatism law, which had the advantage of targeting only Muslims. In the context of such generalized rot, there was no shortage of opportunities for a particular news item or story to be transformed into a "moral advantage" in the hands of a desperate government. This is what happened with the murder of police officer Éric Masson and the huge demonstration of radicalized police that followed. In this case, a real crime blown out of proportion by police unions, the media, and the most reactionary political field (all the statistics disprove the notion that there has been an increase in crime against law enforcement) tipped the

---

10   TN: Nuit Debout (variously translated as "Up All Night," "Standing Night," or "Rise up at Night") is a social movement that began on March 31, 2016, arising out of protests against proposed labor reforms known as the El Khomri law (*Loi travail*).

11   TN: "La loi 'sécurité globale,'" or the "global security bill passed by the French Parliament in April 2021, extending surveillance and police powers, and criminalizing the dissemination of images identifying police officers in operation. The legislation was widely protested again and criticized by human rights and media organizations.

ecologist and Communist Party leaders toward Zemmour and De Villiers's side. This was a total victory for the fascists, and a disaster for the left, which remained stunned and speechless. On a national level, the "moral advantage" was fully in effect.

Only Mélenchon tried to salvage his honor as he clung to a sinking ship. With blind faith, he found his way to Damascus. He took a risk: he got his hands dirty. To side with the Muslims means having to risk taking responsibility for the next bloodshed perpetrated by one of their own; it means suffering the wrath of the "moral advantage" off of which the opposing party will profit. I once told an indigenous person, traumatized by the risk of cooptation, that Mélenchon was a "spoil of war." That there was a part of us and of our struggles in him. The expression did not escape me.

During his presidential campaign, when a journalist asked him whether the children of jihadists held in Syria should be repatriated, he gave this astonishing reply, which I am quoting from memory here: "Yes, we must retrieve 'our little ones.'"[12] Their parents must be judged and punished, but the children must be repatriated.

Our little ones. The same words used by the lady who loves her children so much took on a diametrically opposed meaning.

Our little ones. Not only do the children of terrorists (whatever side they're on) remain children, they are also Mélenchon's children, the children of a France he proposes to lead. Mélenchon loves other people's children. Better still, he loves the children of his enemies. Because children, he says, are not responsible for their parents' actions. What gives this moment its grace is that he is speaking from his heart and mind; he is human, calm, indifferent to the ambient noise.

The proof of the pudding is in the eating.

The proof of indigenous autonomy is in the 2019 March against Islamophobia. Mélenchon and [Philippe] Martinez were there. Spoils of war. How long will it take to conquer them? Twenty years? Thirty years? It must be said that the far right gave us quite a leg up.

---

12   Jean-Luc Mélenchon, on the set of *C dans l'air*, on France 5, January 30, 2022.

A few days earlier, they had attacked a mosque. The "moral advantage" backfired on Bruckner. No cause for celebration, but this time it worked in our favor. It must be said that political antiracism also played a part: this is how we know that Islamophobia is the conjunctural weapon of the colonial counter-revolution, a form of racism that targets the poorest part of the French proletariat. That it is used to rebuild unity among Whites, specifically, between elite France and lower-class France against the lowest class. In short, that it is a key element in the service of the integral racial State and the fascism that lies in ambush. Mélenchon and Martinez finally understood this. Rejoice.

Can we trust them now?

What a mistake that would be. Our ancestor told us: "There are no allies by divine right."[13]

The great and miraculous march against Islamophobia of 2019 was like a prefiguration of the alliance between rednecks and barbarians. The workers' organizations came to us. They acknowledged us. There were tears, lots of emotions. But the march was an ogress. It devoured the decolonial movement. Indigenous autonomy? Vampirized. Vanished into thin air. That was the deal: "Yes, but on the condition that …"

On the condition that the autonomous fringes are ousted, on the condition that you submit to the narrative of the Republic and its universalism, on the condition that you respect the agenda of the reformist left, on the condition that you put water in your tea … in short, on the sole condition of your subordination.[14]

The ancestor's words resonate in our heads. We must "distinguish between alliance and subordination."[15] And here we are again, stripped bare. We (almost) have to start all over again. Regain the advantage. I only hope that past experiences and decolonial polit-

---

13   Aimé Césaire, in his letter of resignation to the PCF: "Letter to Maurice Thorez (October 24, 1956)," trans. Chike Jeffers, *Social Text* 103: 28, no. 2 (Summer 2010): 151.

14   "March contre l'islamophobie du 10 novembre 2019: un autre bilant," Parti des Indigènes de la République, January 7, 2020.

15   TN: Césaire, "Letter to Maurice Thorez," 149.

ical theory don't just go up in smoke. They have taught us this: we must always be cautious with Whites, whether bourgeois or petty, and their organizations and various forms of representation. No complacency, no paranoia. We're with them when we have to be, against them when we have to be, separate from them when we have to be. In other words, we must build a political strategy that goes beyond both separatism and assimilationism. With, against, separately, we move toward the Great Alliance, toward the decolonial majority. FACTS.

"If things were as they should be, the most conscientious of you would be tasked with making us a proposition to avoid the worst. But things are not as they should be. It is incumbent on us to fulfill this task."[16]

So be it. But I must warn the reader that what follows applies only to those who consent to impurity and to getting splashed with shit.

"ALL TOGETHER NOW!"[17]

FACTS. To imagine an alliance between rednecks and barbarians, we have to stop lying to ourselves and take into consideration the asymmetry of affects.

I'll pick up from where I left off in the previous chapter. "Rednecks," on the whole, don't give a damn about racism and the police repression of the indigenous. "Barbarians" are ambivalent, but not without a certain sense of solidarity, when these very "rednecks" are also, like them, being preyed on by the cops. The former don't care about imperialism and its ravages, while the latter suffer from them. The reader must, as I do, appreciate the difficulty of this challenge, which consists in drawing an improbable, unifying line to connect the working classes of advanced capitalist countries. Five centuries of civilization, 150 years of colonial nationalism,

---

16 Houria Bouteldja, *Whites, Jews, and Us: Toward a Politics of Revolutionary Love*, trans. Rachel Valinsky (South Pasadena, CA: Semiotext(e), 2016), 48.

17 TN: "Tous ensemble, tous ensemble, ouais, ouais!" a popular protest chant, but also a reference to Johnny Hallyday's 2022 song "Tous Ensemble," the official anthem of the French soccer team during that year's FIFA World Cup.

some seventy years of colonial counter-revolution, and forty years of rising white supremacism are watching us. Yet, as I write these lines, and against all odds, an equally improbable white left is rising. It is breaking with the Islamophobic consensus, with the identitarian consensus, with the security consensus, with repressive policies against migrants, with the European consensus, with the imperialist consensus. It does so rather limply, but it does so all the same. This white left is at the gates of power, and its program—which is neither revolutionary nor decolonial, but bold nonetheless—far from being an obstacle in its course, is empowering it. There is still such a thing as a French soul. It wafts down to us, vaguely, from the 1789 Revolution, its ideals. It's the still-beating heart of the Commune. We find ourselves reconsidering words. These, for instance: "Liberty, equality, fraternity." Just yesterday, we scorned them, but today, we look at them with fresh eyes. Words that come back to life, swirling, outlining new choreographies. Could it be that the incessant Islamophobic and anti-terrorist bludgeoning did not completely win out over the spirit of the Revolution? A risk is taken: to risk being accused of complicity with terrorism, Islamists, delinquents … Because this left—against all odds—refuses to conflate the inhabitants of the *quartiers* with the murderers of the Bataclan or *Charlie Hebdo*. It's not really up to speed on these issues. It doesn't know how to account for this "minority" of "fanatical" Muslims who "stir shit up," and the "majority" who "respect the laws of the Republic and assimilate." It doesn't have the words, doesn't yet have the right glasses or the courage to wear them. It stands on this weak defense: no conflations! A feeble resistance, but the enemy is not deceived: "Islamo-Leftists!" "Islamo-Bolsheviks!" This will be the new left's punishment for not submitting to the racial consensus. This break with French-style neoconservatism marks a decisive step toward building unity among white and non-white working classes. A point has been scored. But without an organized force, the indigenous will remain tributaries to and dependent on this pusillanimous left. We must persist in returning to the FACTS.

The FACTS are the asymmetry of affects. We can't be "all together" without a communion of indignation, a reciprocity of solidarities, a convergence of interests. It is this lucidity that has set so many militants on the path to political independence. It is this lucidity that has contributed to the transformation of the left and the imposition of a decolonial agenda. Duly noted. And yet, as we have said, this was achieved by liquidating the autonomy and efforts at unification of indigenous power. But let's not dwell on lamentations. A non-negligible portion of the social forces continue to read reality through material, political contradictions (a luxury), while decolonial thought continues to inform and contribute to the reading of social conflicts. We must drive this point home and seek out common interests, unity, the historical bloc. "All together now," sure, but on what platform? As long as we remain incapable of awakening the apathetic body of abstentionists and redefining a new white dignity that can compete with the far right, any attempt at unity between "rednecks" and "barbarians" will seem illusory to me. Not that indigenous dignity is secondary, but the inertia of the former and its demons bear most fatally on the future of the latter. So too must we find an outlet for this dignity other than resignation or racism. This is a priority. The first step is to deprive the ruling bloc of the levers that produce the political errantry and despair of the petty Whites, which the far right uses to gain access to their souls and consolidate its hegemony.

Since we need to conserve our feeble forces and reserve our ammunition, it's important to aim accurately and identify not the enemy—whom we already know—but their Achilles heel. If the longevity of the integral racial State is guaranteed, on the one hand, by its racial arm, and on the other, by its social arm, the flaw in the armor can be quickly located: the European Union. It is the European Union that deprives the white working classes of their destiny, notably through the continuous erosion of their sovereignty and decision-making power. It's the EU that threatens their purchasing power, that pressures them, and hangs them out to dry. It's the EU that betrays the social pact. The EU is the weakest link of the integral State. From now on, we will have to think big, to aim far. At least as far as empire. Our common enemy: the European Union! If this is the case, the only acceptable refuge for the majority of people will be, contrary to all expectations, the nation-state. And if the international character of the subaltern classes is the ultimate horizon, they must first be able to re-nationalize and reroot themselves, in order to gain access to power structures and recreate the conditions for popular hegemony. I'll come back to this in a moment, but first, there is a critical task ahead of us. For no enterprise of this kind, however essential, will succeed if it cannot reach people's souls.

USING UNNECESSARY GESTURES SPARINGLY—AS IN "HOLDING OUR NOSES" ...

And rather than shun Soral's theories (or cruel forms of political Islam), which is based on powerful affects, we must understand its logic in order to turn it on its head. To this end, cries of outrage, "never again," and soliloquies about the belly of the foul beast will be of no avail. To dismantle the Soralian machine (which is already outmoded as a media phenomenon, but far from over as a social reality), we need, if I may be permitted a sentimental departure, to feel a certain tenderness toward "those people." At least enough to be willing to wade through the mud with them and get our hands dirty. However, no software on the political left has been programmed to understand and effectively combat these affects—the need for nationhood and virility—in all their ambivalence and apparent homogeneity.

No theory on the left today is equipped to respond to these needs because they clash with certain fundamental underpinnings of progressive and/or universalist thinking. When the left is internationalist, it doesn't understand the need for nationhood (and hence security); when it is Republican and universalist, it doesn't understand the need for identity and religion. When it is anti-fascist, it fails to understand the harmful consequences of the State's differential treatment of antisemitism and other forms of racism, and when it is feminist, it fails to understand the oppression of non-hegemonic masculinities, whether white or non-white. Whatever the face of this left, it stubbornly insists on providing inadequate analyses and responses, without taking into serious consideration the singularity of subaltern subjects of class or race. And yet, to combat the nationalistic, antisemitic, and sexist perversions of rednecks and barbarians, we need to *understand*—which is not synonymous with "justify" but rather a condition for combating and destroying these base instincts. These two populations have interests that are partly divergent and partly convergent. The indigenous are struggling with an assimilationism that is hampered by State racism. The latter are seeking answers to the degradation of their way of life, which, according to Soral's conspiratorial explanations, should be attributed to "Empire" and to immigrants rather than to a technocratic Europe and unbridled globalization. Of course, none of these questions is easy to answer, because as decolonial activists we will never defend a nationalistic, antisemitic, or patriarchal project that is radically opposed to our ideals of social justice and fraternity. On the other hand, we can imagine drawing on white and non-white subaltern masculinities, and on the working classes' need for nationhood, to create social energies that can be converted into revolutionary projects. To do this, we need to start by respecting the dignity of these masculinities, and of the lower and lowest classes' attachment to the national fact. To abolish these affects, we must first see them for what they are: sites of refuge against the terror of modernity. From there, we must identify what, in the intrinsically heterosexist condition of the nation, pits the bourgeois against the poor, so that we can enter the breach.

The history of the bourgeoisie is one of continual oscillation between identification with and betrayal of the nation. For the nation does not have the same meaning for the bourgeoisie as it does for the working-class and popular masses ...[18]

... who are attached to it because the national-popular form of the State was also imposed by class struggle, workers, peasants, and women ... I claim that Soral, detestable as he is, has taken

---

18 Nicos Poulantzas, *State, Power, Socialism* (London: Verso, 2014 [1978]), 131.

advantage of this "oscillation" of the bourgeoisie and of the authentic relationship that "petty Whites" have to the nation. He was able to connect his discourse to that of class struggle, reaching back far into the history of the people's suffering. White men, women, and children were also, and for a long time, beasts of burden, semislaves, miners condemned to an early death, workers doubly exploited in the factory and at home, uprooted peasants, cannon fodder, cripples, and amputees. Their struggles, their revolts, and their participation in the global workers' aristocracy from the mid-twentieth century onward certainly made them into relatively privileged citizens, spared in some sense from the wars that continue to devastate other worlds. But not all their descendants have reached the higher rungs of the social ladder. While they harbored this hope in the immediate postwar period when the social/racial pact was sealed, and while it was within reach during the Trentes Glorieuses,[19] the 1980s and the infamous turn to austerity soon closed that enchanted parenthesis. The State progressively withdrew from landlocked territories, from the countryside and the peripheries, abandoning entire populations in economically traumatized and devastated areas. The scale of de-unionization and the withdrawal of workers' organizations finally drove these despised petty Whites into the camp of abstention, or to the far right, which was the only party to maintain a human relationship with them, no matter how spurious. They were asked to abandon their land to go get urbanized. But this glosses over the fact that social mobility requires capital, and that familial and territorial space is a space of solidarity and culture. All of this has been a source of great satisfaction for far-right polemicists. The authentic France is the France of the soil, the France that preserves its traditions and identity against the globalized, cosmopolitan France of the large metropolises. Notwithstanding the nationalist right parties' racist subtext and hypocritical populism, an anti-capitalist reading of the

---

19 The "Glorious Thirties," a thirty-year period of economic growth in France between 1945 and 1975, following the end of the Second World War. The term, first used by Jean Fourastié in the book, *Les Trente Glorieuses, ou la révolution invisible de 1946 à 1975* (Paris: Fayard, 1979), is derived from *Les Trois Glorieuses* (the glorious three), three days of revolution from July 27 to 29, 1830, in France.

abandonment of the white working classes cannot escape a rigorous review of the disdain with which the left brushed aside questions of identity and attachment to self that are, contrary to appearances, as moral as they are material. But Soral did something even more remarkable. Through his unequivocal admiration for Islam, and his intuition that Muslims are attached to forms of transcendence that escape modern, secular, and capitalist logic, he experienced his people's cultural wasteland. He put his finger on that notorious cultural insecurity at the root of the petty Whites' existential malaise. The dread experienced in the face of the breakdown of the simple life, of simple relationships, and of simple tastes, and the need for absolute values, all supply the far right's melancholy, which reveals, in the negative, its opponents' emotional callousness. And yet, these are not impossible questions to connect to an emancipatory and radically anti-fascist project. But first we need to revitalize and dialectically rethink our relationship to the nation-state, to identity, to culture, and to the relationship white working classes maintain with the flag. The ultimate aim, of course, being to overcome this relationship, but not without first going through it and its part of light—the light contained in the French Revolution and its betrayed ideals, which continue to live on. It's a risky prospect, riddled with pitfalls. But it is inevitable.

This prompts me to reconsider Zhu Enlai's ironic reply to a French journalist, who asked him what he thought of the French Revolution: "It's too early to tell." Perhaps this was an expression of wisdom rather than mockery.

"LET US LEAVE THIS EUROPE!"[20]

Come, comrades, the European game is finally over, we must look for something else.[21]

---

20 Frantz Fanon, *The Wretched of the Earth*, trans. Richard Philcox (New York: Grove Press, 2004), 235.
21 TN: Ibid., 236.

Fanon was speaking to the colonized at the dawn of the 1960s. And yet, when he says "comrades," is he not really addressing the generic human? White people could have heeded him too. But they didn't, at least not that I know of. In fact, when the French electorate voted "no" to the Treaty establishing a Constitution for Europe (TCE) in 2005, it wasn't because Europe was "[massacring man] at every one of its corners, at every corner of the world,"[22] but because it was preparing to betray the specific human with whom it had made a pact, and to whom it owed protection and prosperity. Unlike the nation-state, the European Union struggles to win the consent of the masses. Why? Because of its fundamentally undemocratic nature, which reinforces the exclusion of the masses from centers of decision making? Because it is nothing but an internationalization of the interests of national bourgeois blocs, their very extension within bureaucratic institutions that deprive the peoples of Europe, and the working classes in particular, of their full sovereignty? While belonging to the nation-state was guaranteed by a social/ racial contract, Europe guarantees only capitalist/racial/imperialist integration. What about the social contract? What about popular sovereignty? The "no" that voters expressed to the Maastricht dictatorship stung. The racial, transnational pact was disintegrating. Not for the best reasons, but morality be damned. After all, it doesn't really matter why some Whites want to leave the EU. From where we stand, we know that we must also appeal to this instinct of self-preservation. Even if these Whites don't have a moral motivation beyond their own class interests, their intelligence and their anguish at being crushed by the neoliberal machine can force them to make the same choices we would make. We could call the space of this encounter: Exit from the EU. This is where a return to the national framework and the possibility of going beyond it could materialize; where popular sovereignty could be reformulated; where a new geopolitics of the world could be redefined, one we could also call the "de-Westernization of international relations." So let us leave this Europe! It doesn't matter if their reasons for leaving are anti-liberal

---

22   Ibid., 235.

or even patently French and ours decolonial; what matters is that we leave it. After that, anything is possible. The worst too, of course. But a wager is only worthwhile if it carries a risk.

So let's be clear from the outset: there's no such thing as an intrinsically "good" or "bad" Frexit. The departure from the EU may well serve a racist and imperialist agenda, as is the case with Boris Johnson and his Brexit. When it comes to the EU, then, we're sort of "stuck" between its structural unreformability, a chauvinist-nationalist critique advanced by the far right, and the exaltation of a "Social Europe" on the left. The latter, however, has the merit of wanting to go after the EU's neoliberal project—which is also hitting the indigenous hard. It can serve as a basis for formulating a general decolonial proposal that takes into account both the interests of the "rednecks" and those of the "barbarians," which are partly convergent and partly divergent.

So we need to "find something else." But what? Fanon doesn't tell us what it is. And we have not, since the African and Asian independences, discovered a magic formula for radically overcoming the political structures born of Western modernity. What remains impossible to topple is the nation-state—the most totalizing State institution, the most deeply rooted in people's consciousness, and the most hated by us.

So why not try to reimagine it, after all? It no longer has a monopoly on political authority, but it remains the ultimate matrix of social equilibrium. Isn't it precisely the refuge frame that has made the Rassemblement National successful and attractive to part of the white proletariat? Setting aside regionalists and internationalists (who are very much in the minority), isn't this the framework that best embodies white dignity? Isn't this the frame of reference through which we could and should compete with the far right? And where do the Barbarians stand in all this? The overwhelming majority, essentially for reasons of race and class, have no particular interest in defending this Europe for the rich, which also proclaims itself white and Christian—but they do have a vested interest in redefining another form of white dignity. If this involves a return to the nation-state—understood as a period of transition toward its overcoming—why not? To sum up: the ultraliberal, bureaucratic, and technocratic European Union deprives the white working classes of their sovereignty. It is in the light of this dispossession that a decolonial politics worthy of the name must consider the question of white dignity, or more precisely, of another white dignity. This politics will necessarily involve getting our hands dirty, because we must reclaim the share that can be directed toward a "national-popular" project from the various forms of nationalism that sometimes don the mask of Republican universalism. This "national-popular" project, as Gramsci suggests, can be articulated to an internationalist concept that we must never lose sight of. To achieve this, we must dare to return to the national framework. Indeed, while the French far right is finding it increasingly difficult to arbitrate between a white, Christian, supremacist Europe and a white, Christian, supremacist nation-state, the white working classes, whether on the far right or the left, are more uncompromising in their relationship with this Europe, which does not guarantee them the same protections and advantages as the nation-state.

The real problem, of course, concerns the relationship between the working class and the modern nation. This profound relationship has to a large extent been underestimated by Marxism, which has continually tended to examine it ... by exclusively referring to the ideological domination of the bourgeoisie.[23]

Some may argue that the nation-state is an instrument of indigenous oppression and imperialist policy par excellence. This is true. However, if we start from the principle that antiracism must be political—that is, that it must raise the question of power in order to fight against the integral racial State—then the possibility of leaving the EU, which is nothing but a racial superstate, becomes unavoidable. It is not a question of whether the national scale is preferable to the European scale, but rather of which scale will enable us to fight most effectively against exploitation and oppression. The absolute lack of

---

23 Poulantzas, *State, Power, Socialism*, 131. TN: Italics in the original, but not in the author's French transcription.

democracy within the EU is the main obstacle to political mobilization on this scale. In fact, such mobilization takes place, first and foremost, within the framework of the State, and it is therefore at the level of the nation-state that the levers of power must be seized—which is quite simply impossible within the framework of the EU, since national policies remain largely determined by it. An exit from the EU is therefore not an end in itself, far from it, but an essential step if the struggle is to progress. I am lying a little when I say that it would only be a step, because the return to the nation-state would be more than a passing phase, and its overcoming a relatively distant horizon toward which we will have to strive, but the conditions for its realization depend largely on whether there exists, on a global scale, a powerful mass utopia. A new idea. A new positive affirmation. Like communism, in the past, or at a more regional scale, political Islam or Pan-Africanism. Without such a revolutionary utopia capable of defying the capitalist monster, the national "phase" may last a while. This is why the return to the nation-state must also be seen as a phase of this utopia, or even as its precondition. We would have to envision both a decolonial strategy for a return to the national framework for indigenous people who don't give a damn about Europe but are in need of a homeland; and an anti-liberal strategy for the white working classes, for whom the homeland is a safe haven as strong and secure as a bar of gold. Why then continue to avoid the politicization of these two opposing and contradictory affects, both of which are nevertheless historically determined by the national/imperial fact? Why not try to find their common denominator? "Rednecks" won't immediately feel concerned by a decolonial Frexit. If a virtuous cycle were to be set in motion, it is an indigenous power balance (comprised of both the indigenous of the interior and of the exterior) that will enable rednecks to be transformed. As things stand, it would be wiser to concentrate on what can attract immediate support and counter the far right's appeal to a public receptive to its ideas, or to simply reawaken interest in politics among those who have dropped out. This would mean politicizing the break with the EU. This would imply defending policies of an economic (the nationalization of strategic sectors of the economy, for example), social, legislative, and cultural (the rehabilitation of regional languages and cultures) nature that could accompany such an exit from the Union. A break with the EU implies a complete reorganization of the State. The return to a national currency, the consequences of which are unknown and uncertain, would nevertheless enable us to regain control of the currently inaccessible levers of monetary policy—a fundamental dimension of popular sovereignty.

To regain control over political and economic decisions—this is a central axis for a Frexit inscribed within a broader anti-liberal policy. This is essential, in fact, if we want to carry out policies that really attack State structures. We can therefore think of "popular" sovereignty, not in terms of the constitutional meaning of the term "people," but as an alliance of subaltern classes and the indigenous within socio-spatial and institutional configurations that borrow from nation-states. Fighting for a *popular Frexit* therefore implies an understanding of sovereignty not as a unilateral concept, but as a relational, and therefore political, concept. Such an alliance between the indigenous and the white working classes could turn a Frexit into an exit that paves the way for a decolonial horizon. Exiting the EU is certainly not a "miracle solution" that will automatically lead us out of the political stagnation revealed by recent health and ecological crises; instead, it is a step within a broader decolonial struggle that includes the Global South and is, today more than ever, indispensable to a global shift in the balance of power.

LET'S MAROON, LET'S MAROON![24]

Because unity will be conflictual, there must be a guarantee of separation. FACTS.

---

24 TN: From Aimé Césaire's poem, "Le verbe marronner" dedicated to René Depestre and first published as "Réponse à René Depestre, poète haïtien (Élements d'un art poétique)" in *Présence Africaine* in 1955. In this version, Césaire writes: "marronnons-les Depestre marronnons-les/comme jadis nous marronnions nos maîtres à fouet." In the 1976 *Oeuvres complètes*, this becomes: "marronnerons-nous Depestre marronnerons-nous?" Clayton Eshleman and Annette Smith translate this line as "shall we escape like slaves Depestre like slaves?" in *The Collected Poetry* (Berkeley, CA: University of California Press, 1983), 368–9. Here, I have preferred to preserve the verb "*marronner*."

A better word to use than separation is independence ... . When you're independent of someone you can separate from them. If you can't separate from them it means you're not independent of them.[25]

Time and again, throughout history, we have been separated from one another; I sense that now we're in a hurry to believe in being "all together." I won't give in to the siren call so quickly. Let us not forget: "In the end, I realized that joining the PC was, in a way, yet another form of resignation."[26] Let's maroon, let's maroon!

FACTS. Independence means autonomy, self-determination. It's the agenda, differed. But it's also about the balance of power that indigenous political power must continue to create with, against, and separately from white forces. "Redneck" power does not exist. It is dispersed across the white political field. It's up to the white revolutionary forces to develop a strategy for them. So too must we turn to them to think the historical bloc in the absence of another organized political alterity. But because it is our primary ally, the left will continue to be our primary opponent, even when it reforms in our favor. We must continue to exert pressure on it. Its affects are not soluble within our own. In times of crisis, the white instinct of self-preservation can swing as far to the left as it can to the right; probably even farther to the right. Whiteness is in decline. Therefore, it is dangerous. What's more, the absence of a decolonial balance of power will increase the capacity of the most reactionary white forces to harm and attract, whereas the existence of an autonomous, structured, and combative indigenous front remains a key factor of unity. The fight against racism and imperialism remains our backbone. We have seen what could make up our common ground. But our antagonisms remain. Autonomy only makes sense if it serves the

---

25 Malcolm X, "Interview by A.B. Spellman," in Malcolm X, *By Any Means Necessary* (New York: Pathfinder, 2008[1970]), 28, 31–2, quoted in Jack Barnes, *Malcolm X: Black Liberation & the Road to Workers Power* (New York: Pathfinder, 2009), 100.

26 Excerpt from the documentary *Césaire contre Aragon*, directed by Guy Deslauriers (2019).

interests of non-Whites first and foremost. Ultimately, this will be a component of the popular sovereignty we need to build, an indispensable condition for a true alliance of rednecks and barbarians. But the indigenous proposal must be more than political or economic; it must be spiritual.

Let's start with what is tangible. And with a simple question: how can we fight against "State racism" if the State in question is not sovereign? A decolonial exit from the EU may not strengthen the French nation-state but, on the contrary, provoke and deepen political fissures within it. A decolonial Frexit could, in fact, be part of the process of overcoming the nation-state. As Sadri Khiari writes:

> The colonial counter-revolution underway is a war to preserve or reinforce the statutory (political, cultural, moral, economic …) domination of one part of the world, a planetary white-European-Christian aristocracy, the "white supermen," as Gramsci put it, over all others.[27]

It is against this "aristocracy" that a decolonial Frexit must fight, unlike the right-wing Brexit, which intended to reinforce white domination via a strengthening of the nation-state. It is important here to point out how the EU directly and deliberately targets indigenous people, not only within the EU but also across the Global South. If France—like other EU member States—has for several years taken a repressive turn, specifically targeting Muslims under the guise of anti-terrorism, this should be considered alongside the EU's "anti-terrorism" directives. As early as 2004, research showed that post-9/11 counterterrorism in European countries was strongly shaped by the EU.[28] We could go even further back: in 1973, with the Copenhagen Declaration on "European identity," European values began to take on a structuring role in European integration. This affirmation of a pseudo-European identity is on par with the debate

---

27 Sadri Khiari, *The Colonial Counter-Revolution in France: From de Gaulle to Sarkozy*, trans. Amos Hodges (South Pasadena, CA: Semiotext(e), 2021), 215.
28 See Liz Fekete's work, especially *A Suitable Enemy: Racism, Migration and Islamophobia in Europe* (London: Pluto Press, 2009).

on national identity during the Sarkozy era. Racial exclusion is at the heart of the European project. And what of the EU's central role in the exploitation of the Global South—facilitated in part through trade agreements, something the Union is uniquely competent in? Recognition of the constitution of the EU as an exploitative bloc is essential if we are to combat the impoverishment of the Global South effectively. A decolonial exit from the Union would therefore be in direct opposition to nationalist exits that are nostalgic for the former colonial empire. On the contrary, a decolonial Frexit must be inscribed within a new political geography, one that involves solidarity and fraternity with the peoples of the South, and dismantles the machinery of exploitation upon which the asymmetrical relations between the EU and the Global South are based.

Exiting the EU will not automatically destroy this "European barricade," but, guided by the right policies, it can contribute to it. An indigenous political power can no longer simply fight against this or that. It must take possession of its full sovereignty and envision the conditions for achieving this sovereignty. To do so, power must be repatriated and kept close at hand.

"O CAPTAIN! MY CAPTAIN"[29]

The reconquest of popular sovereignty must be articulated alongside a strategy for a new popular bloc capable of overturning the balance of power within the integral racial State. This means breaking with racial collaboration. This also implies the consent of the white subaltern classes to this break. Finally, this implies that the break must be desirable. For this to be the case, a solution to the social question will probably not be sufficient. Nor will popular sovereignty. These will be necessary and even indispensable steps, but insufficient in counterbalancing the advantages of whiteness. White dignity must be given a deeper meaning. Whites are not just stomachs to feed or citizens with rights and duties. Whiteness must be redefined. And

---

29   TN: The title of a poem by Walt Whitman's, published in the collection *Leaves of Grass* (1891).

this redefinition, like the return to the nation, will itself be transitional. This is why we need to consider a return to whiteness, while aiming to move beyond it. If it is to be successful, the abolition of race will, I believe, require the reaffirmation of a certain national dignity. Who but Poulantzas understood it better?

> To see the national State as the prize and objective of workers' struggles involves the reappropriation by the working class of its own history. To be sure, this cannot be achieved without the transformation of the State; but it also points to a certain permanency of the State, in its national aspect, during the transition to socialism—permanency not just in the sense of a regrettable survival, but also in that of a positive necessity for the transition to socialism.[30]

This may ruffle the feathers of any self-respecting internationalist, but it is true that national sentiment will never be extinguished by kind words or good feelings. For us, it's quite simple. As a race that has been crushed, we have a right to feel pride, precisely because this pride has been wounded. For Whites, it's trickier, because whiteness is essentially a relationship of domination. In this case, we must go look inside the white person, where there is often an oppressed being, for the luminous part to exalt, even if this means enduring their brandishing of the red, white, and blue flag and the Marseillaise. After all, who gives the anthem and the flag their ultimate meaning? Nothing is stopping petty Whites from imbuing it with revolutionary meaning! What is critical is that they decide, in good faith, who of the indigenous or the ruling classes made them what they are. Who pauperized them? Who abandoned them? Who sold off their culture and traditions? Then, as has already been noted, the critical alliance will take the form of an encounter between, and cohabitation of, the RWB flag and all the indigenous flags. On the Champs-Elysées, for example, during the World Cup won by a

---

30 Poulantzas, *State, Power, Socialism*, 133.

"Black, Black, Black" team. Amid the general jubilation. Didn't we survive that? We were happy, even.

But this hegemonization of popular authority must itself draw its energy from the construction of a unity whose conflictuality will be reinforced, prolonged, and crystallized in race relations: the sovereignty of the white working classes, on the one hand, and indigenous sovereignty, on the other. Of course, like Penelope, we can expect a gradual, linear harmonization of these multitudes, and hope that they will naturally find their way to the construction of the historical bloc. Or, more pragmatically, we might consider that the strategy of power rests on a political direction. This is the approach I favor. But what I am talking about here, to be more precise, is a protean political approach that incorporates conflictuality, differential space-times, and the profound contradictions that exist not only between the two major racial groups (Whites and non-Whites), but also within them. Equipped with this awareness, it is clear that the political leadership of the indigenous cannot be delegated to any white leadership. Indigenous political leadership will have to act strategically to unite the working classes, while scrupulously defending the collective interests of non-Whites, both nationally and internationally, as this is the group most vulnerable to and most easily sacrificed by political forces. As such, it can in no way afford to indulge in promises of a revolution to come. Last but not least, indigenous power will be at the forefront of what we might call the "rehumanization of relations with the world" if we're being a bit idealistic, or "anti-imperialism" if we're not. Indeed, if for Whites there is the right and the left, for us there is the Global South. Of this we are certain: it is on the South that our liberation will depend, from the South that the New Idea will come. That's why indigenous power, alongside the most anti-imperialist white forces and our white brothers and sisters—who we hope will be as numerous as possible—will play a leading role in the project to overcome the nation-state and, hopefully, fraternize with the wretched of the earth.

That is, if they can forgive us.

ASIDE

How many children are born, in this country, of love stories between rednecks and the bourgeoisie?

They exist, but they're fairly rare.

And how many children are born of love stories between barbarians and bourgeois women?

Zohra, Rachida Dati's daughter.

And how many children are born of love stories between rednecks and barbarians?

Many.

Choosing Our Ancestors

It may be that France now has to choose between her attachment to her Empire and the need to have a soul of her own again.[1]

—Simone Weil

A friend from Benin recently said to me: "With all their talk of integration and those infamous 'ancestors the Gauls,' there's a risk that tomorrow we will end up saying 'our ancestors the slavers.'"[2] Damn! Could Malika Sorel—appointed by Sarkozy to the High Council for Integration—have been right when she summarized things as follows: "Immigrating means changing your genealogy"? Suddenly, something like an apparition seemed to emerge out of the fear my friend had expressed.

Let's take a closer look at two historical victims of white supremacy, themselves converted into defenders of white supremacy: Alain Finkielkraut and Éric Zemmour. Both are Jews, of Polish and Algerian origin respectively, and as such, victims of Nazism and collaboration, in the case of the former, and colonization in the case of the latter. We can venture to say that in the future, there will be Black, Arab, and Muslim clones of this ilk, whose appearance in time was deferred only by their delayed assimilation. To understand the mechanics of their conversion, it is important to understand that they first had to renounce their ancestors in order to then adopt their executioners'. This was not without consequences for the health of their souls. Indeed, the place they occupy today in the political arena marks a break in filiation that could be referred to as "betrayal" if

---

1   Simone Weil, *The Need for Roots: Prelude to a Declaration of Duties towards Mankind*, trans. Arthur Wills (London: Routledge, 2002), 165. First published by Editions Gallimard, Paris, in 1949.

2   Ahmad Nougbo, Pan-African militant.

one is located in the camp of the persecuted and uprooted Jews; or as "assimilation" if one is located in the camp of the reactionary Republican ideology on the rise today. As champions of the French neoconservative camp, and even of fascism, these two media personalities prove Nicolas Sarkozy's point when he declared, in 2016: "When you become French, your ancestors are Gallic."

Éric Zemmour goes even further: "To be French, you have to have Napoleon as your ancestor and Jeanne d'Arc as your great-grandmother." He adds:

I'm nostalgic for the time when France dominated Europe, and I understand true nationalists like Putin or Trump. I understand what Putin means very well when he says that anyone who doesn't long for the Soviet Union doesn't have a heart. I think anyone who doesn't long for the Napoleonic Empire isn't really French. I'm nostalgic for the greatness of my country.[3]

But why stop there? Zemmour wants to rehabilitate Marshal Pétain, who made a pact with Hitler in 1940 and collaborated in the deportation of the Jews. After all, he is merely extending the attitude of all those good Republicans who have never ceased to reduce this moment to a "parenthesis," an "accident" in French history, and who have denied "the Republican origins of Vichy."

Subtler still, Alain Finkielkraut reinterprets Sarkozy: "Our ancestors belong to everyone."[4]

This proposition, which has a neoconservative ring coming from the philosopher's mouth, bears an uncanny resemblance to C. L. R. James's decolonial statement: "These are my ancestors, these are my people. They are yours too, if you want them."[5]

Like the West Indian intellectual, Finkielkraut offers us "his" ancestors. This is disturbing. But the discomfort fades as the fog

---

3 "Éric Zemmour répond à l'invitation de Louis Aliot en campagne pour les municipales de 2020," *Made in Perpignan*, September 24, 2019.
4 Alain Finkielkraut, quoted by Élisabeth Levy on the radio show, "L'esprit de l'escalier," Radio RCJ, September 25, 2016.
5 TN: C. L. R. James, "The Making of the Caribbean People," in *Spheres of Existence: Selected Writings* (Westport, CT: Lawrence Hill & Co., 1980), 187.

lifts. Indeed, C. L. R. James offers up his ancestors, but not "all" his ancestors. Only those who fought against slavery. It is not a question of ideological, ethnic, or biological lineage, but rather of a lineage of struggle against infamy. As for Finkielkraut, he indiscriminately offers up *all* (or almost all) his ancestors, from Vercingetorix to Charles de Gaulle and his Algerian War, by way of Napoleon the executioner of Europe and Thiers the murderer of the Paris Commune. Sarkozy/Finkielkraut's proposal is diametrically opposed to James's. The former is characterized by its identitarian and colonial nationalism, whereas the latter is characterized by its revolutionary life force. While the former encompasses a broad spectrum, ranging from the Socialist Party to neoconservatives, the latter struggles to make its way within the political landscape, where it is caught between Republicanism and a radical leftism that remains resistant to the prism of race as an analytic and political category. Yet, like Monsieur Jourdain[6] who speaks prose without knowing it, the radical left produces white race without knowing it. Granted, unlike the intellectuals in proximity to power, the radical left is sorting through its historical references. Of course, it prefers Rosa Luxemburg to Joan of Arc and Louise Michel to Victor Hugo, but it also has blinders on. The radical left still prefers Robespierre to Toussaint Louverture—even though the Haitian Revolution extends and strengthens the French Revolution—just as it prefers the great figures of the French Resistance to Algerian figures, who are always a little dubious, a little suspicious, a little barbaric. By failing to understand and accept James's proposition, white revolutionaries deprive themselves of everything, especially their souls.

Luckily, the indigenous are one step ahead. They carry their souls with them everywhere they go.

The "battle of the statues"[7] that has been going on for several years and intensified since the death of George Floyd—the toppling

---

6   TN: A reference to the main character in Molière's comédie-ballet, *Le Bourgeois gentilhomme* (*The Bourgeois Gentleman*), 1670.

7   TN: See, for instance, Hamid Dabashi, "The Battle of the Statues: Rewriting World History," Aljazeera, July 9, 2020, last accessed June 11, 2024, www.aljazeera.com/opinions/2020/7/9/the-battle-of-the-statues-rewriting-world-

of Cecil Rhodes's statue in South Africa, of Edward Colston's in Bristol, of Victor Schoelcher's in Martinique, or the graffitiing of Colbert's statue in Paris—refutes the inevitability of the Gallic myth. In France and in the West, decolonial forces are resisting the injunction to assimilate, in particular by attacking symbols of colonialism and slavery. This is a notable step forward, for these ongoing acts of toppling are neither marginal nor anecdotal. They are the expression of a decolonial consciousness in the making capable of identifying the ideological basis of white power, founded on the law of the strongest and a history written by the victors. Historical figures whose virtue is not so much to exalt the past as it is to confirm the current world order and, we have cause to fear, prepare the future. Toppling is no longer just a symbolic act. By deciding to recover historical truth and impose the perspective of the "wretched of the earth," it becomes a powerful political act with the capacity to challenge official myths. Duly noted. And then what?

I said, they carry the soul.

Duly noted. And what else? Faith.

And? A sense of community.

What else?

The topplers, the believers, the communitarians are whitewashed natives. Integrated into the social pact in a subordinate position, but integrated nonetheless. Neither white nor wretched of the earth. How, then, can they truly rid themselves of their "Gallic ancestors"? The truth is that, together with the "person of French stock," they form a "national community"; if they dare to deny it, they must explain themselves, they must come clean! Why do they stay? WHY? This is the sadistic, spiteful question Lepenists ask—a question that bears some relevance because it is so disconcerting to us.

My friend's hypothesis is confirmed. If we are, objectively, heirs of the Gauls, why shouldn't we also be heirs of the slavers, since we too profit off of the colonial epic? Our ancestors, the slavers ... they

history#:~:text=In%20the%20US%2C%20the%20battle,generals%20of%20the%20Confederate%20army.

barbarize us.[8] The fascists are right, in a way. We have to own up to the crime with them.

On the other hand, the vast majority of white people, with their phantasmagorical Gallic ancestors, never seem to identify with indigenous struggles, and even less with their liberation figures, who remain irredeemably "other." Toussaint Louverture was a liberator of slaves, not slaveholders; Hô Chi Minh, a liberator of Vietnamese people; and the FLN, a liberator of Algerians. And yet, as Sartre would argue, every victory, every advance in the anti-colonial struggle has helped to "debarbarize" white people. Every setback, to rebarbarize them.

This, in short, is what we must strive for: accelerating the debarbarizarion of white people and decelerating the barbarization of indigenous people. There are many reenchanting ancestors who could contribute to this project and populate this pantheon: Sitting Bull, Geronimo, Cochise, Solitude, Toussaint Louverture, Nat Turner, Harriet Tubman, John Brown, Robespierre, Saint Just, Emir Abdelkader, Omar al-Mokhtar, Lalla Fatma N'Soumer, Louise Michel, Patrice Lumumba, Hô Chi Minh, Lenin, Mandela, Malcolm X, Larbi Ben M'hidi, Ernesto Guevara, Martin Luther King, Fernand

---

8   TN: The term "barbarize" here only partially arrives at the meaning and contemporary connotations of the French *ensauvager*. Historically, the verb *ensauvager* (or *ensauvagir*) is associated with the stigmatization of native and later enslaved peoples as *savages* (and the notion of the "noble savages"). In the 1950s, Aimé Césaire turned the term against itself in a denunciation of colonialism; he writes of "*ensauvagement*" to describe the slow and steady process by which the colonizer becomes "decivilized" by the "poison" colonization itself has spread (Joan Pinkham translates the term as "proceed[ing] toward *savagery*" in the 2000 edition of *Discourse on Colonialism*, published by Monthly Review Press, 36). Since the 1970s, neoconservatives and the far right have variously deployed the concept of *ensauvagement* to stoke nationalistic and Islamophobic sentiment, and sound the alarm on immigration, the rise of violence and petty crime, and anti-white racism. In 2020, political debates over the term erupted after Marine Le Pen and Minister of the Interior, Gerald Darmanin, publicly decried the "*ensauvagement* of French society." For a brief summary of the history and recent polemics around this term, see Norimitsu Onishi and Constant Méheut, "A Coded Word from the Far Right Roil's France's Political Mainstream," *New York Times*, September 3, 2020, last accessed June 11, 2024, www.nytimes.com/2020/09/04/world/europe/france-ensauvagement-far-right-racism.html.

Iveton, Marek Edelman, Simone Weil, Ghassan Kanafani, Yasser Arafat, Thomas Sankara, Abd al-Karim al-Khattabi, Toni Morrison, Jean Genet ... And so many more.

However, this list could not be complete without a thought for the memory of the Unknown soldier. Admittedly, as a soldier of Empire, he is in no way comparable to the heroes and heroines of the anti-colonial struggle, but his instrumentalization by the nationalist narrative interpellates us, first because it is not uncommon to hear the indigenous bemoan that their grandparents also died at Verdun or on the Chemin des Dames—as if this earned them a certificate of Frenchness—but also because this instrumentalization freezes the Unknown as a soldier, to the detriment of his class allegiance and perhaps, yes, his ... race.

Every possible thing has been imagined about him, including his wife, who is even more unknown than him. The nationalistic propensity constraining our imaginations, however, prevents us from daring to imagine that he might have been Black, Arab, or Indochinese. And yet, what if he were? The little village girl in Tavernier's film, *Life and Nothing But* (1989), her ingenuousness, nearly hints at this. Colonial troops fought in the war, they were in the outposts. Who could identify, with any certainty, a body torn to shreds and say that it is neither a "Kraut," an "Arab," or a "Negro"?

Bertolt Brecht's poem "Guidance for the People on Top" (1927)[9] invites us to do just that, by taking the path of disidentification of the Unknown. Why celebrate the Unknown Soldier, he asks? Here, in its entirety, is Alain Badiou's remarkable commentary:

Brecht talks about the most famous collective and State ceremonial of the last century concerning death: the celebration of the unknown soldier, all over the world, during all the years following the slaughter of 1914–1918 .... [A]fter having massacred millions in the mud and snow, with such a null result that it had to be done

9   TN: Bertold Brecht, "Guidance for the People on Top," trans. Frank Jellinek, in *Bertold Brecht: Plays, Poetry and Prose*, ed. John Willett and Ralph Manheim (London: Eyre Methuen, 1976), 129–30.

again twenty years later, the imperial powers frequently invited their people to prostrate themselves before the remains of a corpse so damaged that no one could recognize it: an anonymous dead man. The point that Brecht addresses is the introduction of the adjective "unknown" into the nationalist ceremonial. He asks: why celebrate the unknown soldier? The unknown soldier is such only insofar as national finitude captures his poor remains. He thus becomes, *nolens volens*, an unknown perfectly classified in the categories of finitude, a homegrown unknown, an unknown whose value is strictly based on his nationality. To the fact that it is out of passion for his nation—in truth out of obedience to the orders of the State—that he died, blown up, torn apart, buried in the mud, without it being possible to identify what remained of him. The word "unknown," Brecht remarks, is insidiously contradicted by the supposedly shared knowledge of the value of imperial national identity. He is the unknown of this nation; the unknown of this empire. The poor dead man, shredded and unnamed, is asked to embody, in front of the flag of the ceremony, the fact that it is right to die for this national idea. Unknown designates a body all the more devoted to national celebration, a body devoured by the power of the State, a body that is in no way known or recognized on the basis of its singular existence, but only in that it symbolizes national identity in the register of death—a register here that is the accomplice of identitarian passion. Then Brecht is going to present us another unknown, one whom Marx very early on announced precisely had no fatherland ("the proletarians have no fatherland"). Who was without identity. Who embodied what Marx called generic humanity: the worker of all the cities of the world. This is how Brecht describes this unknown worker, who should be contrasted with the unknown soldier: an ordinary man, pulled out of the mesh of traffic, whose face has not been seen, whose secret being has not been glimpsed, whose name has not been distinctly heard. And he calls him the *Unknown Worker*, the worker of the great cities on the teeming continents. It is to him, to him alive, that we should finally pay tribute. What Brecht wants is to free the unknown from any other identity than universal. It would be to internationalize him, the unknown, to tear him away from the mortifying national passions. It would be to link the "unknown" to the affirmation of generic humanity, in its journey toward communism, instead of welding this word, "unknown," to death and to the orders of the State. It would be to make millions of unknown living people into the real substance of the future rather than into the tense and emaciated symbol of the rivalries between States. Yes, the celebration of the unknown worker could be for internationalism what the Feast of the Federation was for the French Revolution: the collective, organized consciousness, on a world scale, of the fact that a new world is on the agenda, one in which the political hero is in some sense this nobody, whom nobody knows, and whom everybody knows is the only force available to continue the construction of the new world. Brecht writes: "Such a man should / in the interest of us all / Be commemorated by a substantial ceremony / With a broadcast tribute / 'To the Unknown Worker' / And / A Stoppage of work by the whole of humanity / Over the entire planet." We see that there is not only, in the passage from the unknown soldier to the unknown worker, the transformation of a closed identity symbol into a universal figure, not only the dialectical shift from the cult of death and the past to that of life and the future. There is also the restitution of popular actions to their true recipient: to the false strike, to the false minute of silence imposed by the State, is substituted the idea of a world workers' solidarity, celebrating its own generic value. In truth, to the finitude of the trio Death-Nation-State is substituted, by this variation on the adjective "unknown," a potential infinity for which "worker" is the provisional name, and which is like the invention, by humanity, of its immanent truth.[10]

---

10   Alain Badiou, "Comment vivre et penser en un temps d'absolue désorientation?" (How to live and think in a time of absolute disorientation?" lecture, La Commune, Aubervilliers, France, October 4, 2012, posted on October 14, 2012, YouTube video, 1:18:46, www.youtube.com/watch?v=b6iNwSQTVkc. Translation adapted from the transcription by François Duvert, last accessed June 11, 2024, www.entretemps.asso.fr/Badiou/4-10-2021-anglais.pdf.

This brilliant analysis does not miss its mark. We are literally transported. Almost completely won over. But only almost, because a certain bafflement persists for the indigenous. How does being a worker exonerate the soldier and enable him to access generic humanity? Aren't Brecht—and Badiou—getting ahead of themselves? Haven't they skipped over all the steps before the ascension of white workers to generic humanity? What is the wretched of the earth to think of this generous proposal when the aforementioned worker receives only the crumbs of plunder, when defense of the homeland is part of the imperialist gambit? Why would generic humans agree to a worldwide commemoration of this unknown person on the sole basis that he is a worker, when the wretched of the earth see him first and foremost as white? And finally, why would the working-class condition in the heart of empire be the right starting point from which to extend the universal? The undoubtedly generous, though still ethnocentric dimension of this proposal, is clear. It's hard to imagine its concrete realization, for there's certainly a step missing. But let's carry on with Brecht. The Unknown soldier is not a soldier but a worker. Okay, why not. But perhaps he's an infantryman of empire? Who can say? What we know for sure is that Captain Perrin could not have returned with the body of a German, a "Negro," or an "Arab." But because this body was so torn to shreds, doubt is permitted. And in this, the subversive nature of this quality of the Unknown suddenly becomes apparent. Because he is Unknown, the State can nationalize him at it pleases; because he is Unknown, Communists can treat him first and foremost as a worker. But what if History were playing a great practical joke on us, and the Unknown were in fact a Barbarian? A new ancestor would be revealed to us, then, an ancestor with the power to reconcile the lower classes, to unite them against the elites. An ancestor with whom we could all identify as the ultimate victims of the capitalist/ imperialist order that has produced us all, some as the wretched of the earth, others as the exploited working class, and all as cannon fodder. A synthesizing ancestor. An ancestor who could reveal our common enemy and shine a light on its face. For the infantryman is also the one who contributed, through his sacrifice, to liberating the

French, in spite of himself and against his own interests. This moral debt will be erased as soon as he is made an ancestor, a gesture by which white people will fully recognize him as a victim. As *their* victim. This is the only way the French can obtain the pardon of the Unknown infantryman and reenter generic humanity.

From beyond the grave, the Unknown infantryman demands the pay that France refuses him. His children and grandchildren survive him on this earth. Anyone with a soul can hear him. He is my ancestor. He could be the ancestor of all French people, but especially of all the petty Whites, whose forebears transferred to him their blood tax.

All it takes is a soul ...

While we wait to unravel the mystery of the Unknown, whose true identity is known only to God, and so that our love story can begin under the best possible auspices, it would be worthwhile, before the tribunal of History, to consider the possibility of his colonial origins. As soon as we have made him a common ancestor, the clear dividing line between Them and Us will appear. It is then that the claws of the all-encompassing racial State will unclench and that the hope of witnessing the end of *this world* will ... perhaps ... return.

For now, let us be silent and cede the floor to the poet.

> You're like a scorpion, my brother,
> you live in cowardly darkness
>   like a scorpion.
> You're like a sparrow, my brother,
> always in a sparrow's flutter.
> You're like a clam, my brother,
> closed like a clam, content,
> And you're frightening, my brother,
>   like the mouth of an extinct volcano.
> Not one,
> not five-
> unfortunately, you number millions.
> You're like a sheep, my brother:

when the cloaked drover raises his stick,
     you quickly join the flock
and run, almost proudly, to the slaughterhouse.
I mean you're [the] strangest creature on earth—
even stranger than the fish
that couldn't see the ocean for the water.
And the oppression in this world
     is thanks to you.
And if we're hungry, tired, covered with blood,
and still being crushed like grapes for our wine,
     the fault is yours—
I can hardly bring myself to say it,
but most of the fault, my dear brother, is yours.[11]

11   Nâzim Hikmet Ran, "The Strangest Creature on Earth," 1947, last accessed June 11, 2024, www.marxists.org/subject/art/literature/nazim/strangestcreature. html.

Acknowledgements

First and foremost, I would like to thank Jean Morisot and Stella Magliani-Belkacem from La Fabrique, for their trust and friendship.

Pluto Press, which has done me the honor of publishing this book in English, and Rachel Valinsky, for her remarkable translation.

Selim Nadi, Daniel Blondet, Félix Boggio, Éwanjé-Épée, Sylvain Jean, and Patrick Bobulesco, my comrades and friends, who listened to me, helped me, and supported me in the writing of this book.

And finally, my whole tribe of rednecks and barbarians, from Paroles d'honneur to Dany and Raz, by way of Ramon Grosfoguel and all my fellow travelers, past and present.

Translator's Acknowledgements

I would like to extend great thanks to the many friends, informants, and thought partners who offered insights, encouragement, and community while working on this translation. To Edwin Nasr, in particular, for the dialogue and critical reading of several drafts; to Matt Longabucco for the attentive comments; to Morgan Bassichis, Kirsten Gill, and Hedi El Kholti for the valuable help along the way. To Neda Tehrani at Pluto Press for the supportive editing. And to Houria, of course, for the work and the trust, thank you.

Index

white supremacism 3, 24, 62, 70,
    87, 96–7, 99, 139, 147, 156
white working class 30, 82, 129
workers
    specialized workers (OS) 78, 80,
    82
    undocumented workers 83–4
working class 41–2, 61
    see also white working class

World Bank 35
World Cup (2018) 153–4

X, Malcolm 130, 160

Zemmour, Éric 102, 136, 156–7
Zhu Enlai 144
Zionism 70

The Pluto Press Newsletter

Hello friend of Pluto!

Want to stay on top of the best radical books
we publish?

Then sign up to be the first to hear about our
new books, as well as special events,
podcasts and videos.

You'll also get 50% off your first order with us
when you sign up.

Come and join us!

Go to bit.ly/PlutoNewsletter

Thanks to our Patreon subscriber:

Ciaran Kane

Who has shown generosity and comradeship in support of our publishing.

Check out the other perks you get by subscribing to our Patreon – visit patreon.com/plutopress.

Subscriptions start from £3 a month.